OVERMAN

THE INTERMEDIARY BETWEEN THE HUMAN AND THE SUPRAMENTAL BEING

Georges Van Vrekhem

OVERMAN

The Intermediary
Between the Human
and the Supramental Being

Georges Van Vrekhem

The works of Sri Aurobindo and the Mother © Sri Aurobindo Ashram

Cover photo courtesy NASA/Ben Smegelsky

ISBN 978-1477524787

Copyright © Georges Van Vrekhem 2012, 2001

All rights reserved.

No part of this publication may be reproduced, stored in a retrieval system, or transmitted, in any form or by any means, electronic, mechanical, photocopying, recording or otherwise, without the prior permission of the publishers.

This edition is not for sale in India

Contents

Author's Note	7
1. An Encounter in Sleepy Pondicherry	11
2. Four Pillars	20
3. Turning Towards the Earth	44
4. A First Sketch of Supermanhood	73
5. Overman	110
6. The Consciousness of the Overman	146
Note About the Sources	167
Biographical Note	168

For Mia Berden and Carel Thieme,
who helped when help was needed

Author's Note

Sri Aurobindo and the Mother wrote and spoke at a time before the awareness of "gender specific language". Yet, they more than anybody else stood for the importance and dignity of the individual in all its aspects, male and female. For those who are not familiar with their personalities and their work, it may suffice to say that they admitted in their Ashram sadhaks and sadhikas on an equal footing at a time when this was most unusual.

When writing on subjects in connection with Sri Aurobindo and the Mother it is not always possible, however hard one tries, to adapt one's language to the present sensibilities.

The book before you offers an important new presentation of an aspect of Sri Aurobindo and the Mother's vision and yogic development. The Mother's French term *surhomme*, meaning the intermediary between the human and the supramental being, has until now been wrongly translated as "superman", the word which in Sri Aurobindo and the Mother's work stands throughout for the supramental being. To end this confusion and to clearly indicate the place the intermediary being occupies in the ongoing evolution beyond humankind, I find it essential to translate *surhomme* as "overman".

Georges Van Vrekhem

In the untransformed part of humanity itself there might well arise a new and greater order of mental human beings: for the directly intuitive or partly intuitivised but not yet gnostic mental being, the directly or partly illumined mental being, the mental being in direct or part communion with the higher-thought plane would emerge: these would become more and more numerous, more and more evolved and secure in their type, and might even exist as a formed race of higher humanity leading upwards the less evolved in a true fraternity born of the sense of the manifestation of the One Divine in all beings.

Sri Aurobindo: *The Life Divine*, p. 999

It might be that the psychological change, a mastery of the nature by the soul, a transformation of the mind into a principle of light, of the life-force into power and purity would be the first approach, the first attempt to solve the problem, to escape beyond the merely human formula and establish something that could be called a divine life upon earth, a first sketch of supermanhood, of a supramental living in the circumstances of the earth-nature ... It would not be the total transformation, the fullness of a divine life in a divine body. There would be a body still human and indeed animal in its origin and fundamental character and this would impose its own inevitable limitations on the higher parts of the embodied being.

Sri Aurobindo: *Essays in Philosophy and Yoga*, pp. 536-37

It can be affirmed with certainty that there will be an intermediate specimen between the mental and the supramental being, a kind of overman who will still have the qualities and in part the nature of man, which means that he will still belong in his most external form to the human being of animal origin, but that he will transform his consciousness sufficiently to belong, in his realisation and activity, to a new race, a race of overmen.

The Mother: *Questions and Answers* 1957-58, p. 277

1.
An Encounter in Sleepy Pondicherry

And Thy reign shall be indeed established upon earth[1]

– the Mother

On 29 March 1914, a Parisian lady in Pondicherry went around 3 p.m. from the *Hôtel d'Europe* in the Rue Suffren to no. 41 Rue François Martin. She was Madame Mirra Richard and she had arrived with her husband, Paul, in the sleepy colonial port that very morning. The Richards had boarded the Japanese ship *Kagu Maru* in Marseilles three weeks earlier, sailed through the Suez Canal up to Colombo, crossed the Palk Strait, boarded the Boat Mail at Danushkodi and arrived safely at their exotic destination.

Paul Richard was a philosopher and a politician. He had first come to Pondicherry four years earlier in order to support a local candidate during the elections for the Chamber of Deputies in Paris. As a French territory, Pondicherry was entitled to two representatives. Richard, however, was also deeply interested in occultism and religion, and his main reason for having travelled to the South Indian town may well have been that he wanted to meet an Indian yogi. In this he had been extraordinarily lucky, for Aurobindo Ghose, the well-known freedom fighter turned yogi, had just arrived in Pondicherry, looking for a safe haven from the British authorities who wanted to arrest him, "the most dangerous man in India", at any cost. Richard had been deeply impressed by Aurobindo Ghose and had told his wife about him. The reason she accompanied Richard on his second visit to Pondicherry may well have been that he wished

---

1. The Mother: *Prayers and Meditations*, p. 124.
(See the note about the sources at the back of the book.)

her to meet Aurobindo Ghose. Richard's aim was to get himself elected as a Deputy, but in this he would not succeed.

It would be an exaggeration to say that Mirra had been enthusiastic about undertaking the voyage. On 3 March 1914 she wrote in her diary: "As the day of departure draws near, I enter into a kind of self-communion; I turn with a fond solemnity towards all those thousand little nothings around us which have silently, for so many years, played their role of faithful friends: I thank them gratefully for all the charm they were able to give to the outer side of our life". This suggests that they planned to stay abroad for a long time. "Then I turn towards the future and my gaze becomes more solemn still. What it holds in store for us I do not know nor do I care to know."[2] After his first visit to Pondicherry, Paul Richard had brought back a photograph of Aurobindo Ghose and she, despite her advanced occult capacities, had seen only the politician in him.

Therefore, while walking the mile or so from her hotel to the house where Ghose was living with a few companions, all of them Bengali revolutionaries, Madame Richard perhaps had mixed expectations. Paul had already gone out to greet Aurobindo Ghose immediately upon their arrival in the morning; on the occasion of her first meeting with the unknown Indian, Mirra had wanted to see him alone. Expecting nothing, she had nevertheless prepared everything – as we know from her later conversations – and may have been mulling over some thoroughly considered questions in her mind.

There she stood, then, at the bottom of the staircase leading to the first floor, where Aurobindo Ghose was living – and there he stood, at the top: *"Exactly* my vision! Dressed in the same way, in the same position, in profile, his head held high. He turned his head towards me and I saw in his eyes that it was He."[3] For many years Mirra had been visited and guided in her dreams by several masters, one of whom she named Krishna. This "Krishna" always appeared to her in a dress which she, at the time unfamiliar with the Indian *dhoti*, could not identify

---

2. The Mother: *Prayers and Meditations*, p. 93.
3. Sujata Nahar: *The Mother's Chronicles V*, p. 580.

1. An Encounter in Sleepy Pondicherry

and which she therefore thought to be a "costume worn in visions". Now he stood there before her in the flesh, embodied on earth: Aurobindo Ghose.

The significance of the moment became immediately apparent to her, and we read in her diary entry of the next day: "It matters little that there are thousands of beings plunged in the densest ignorance. He whom we saw yesterday is on earth; his presence is enough to prove that a day will come when darkness shall be transformed into light, and Thy reign shall indeed be established upon earth."[4] ("Thy" and "Thou" refer to the Lord, the Divine to whom the diary entries are addressed.) A night had elapsed between the meeting and the entry in her diary, and things were now seen in a certain perspective: "In the presence of those who are integrally Thy servitors, those who have attained the perfect consciousness of Thy presence [in this case Aurobindo Ghose], I become aware that I am still far, very far from what I yearn to realise; and I know that the highest I can conceive, the noblest and purest is still dark and ignorant beside what I should conceive. But this perception, far from being depressing stimulates and strengthens the aspiration, the energy, the will to triumph over the obstacles so as to be at last identified with Thy law and Thy work."[5]

The importance of the encounter is also obvious from the following entries in her diary. 1 April 1914: "I feel we have entered the very heart of Thy sanctuary and grown aware of Thy very will. A great joy, a deep peace reigns in me, and yet all my inner [mental] constructions have vanished like a vain dream and I find myself now, before Thy immensity, without a frame or system, like a being not yet individualised. All the past in its external forms seems ridiculously arbitrary to me, and yet I know it was useful in its own time. But now all is changed: a new stage has begun."[6] 3 April: "It seems to me that I am being born into a new life and all the methods, the habits of the past can no longer be of any use. It seems to me that what I

---

4. The Mother, *Prayers and Meditations*, p. 124.
5. Ibid.
6. Ibid., p. 125.

thought were results are nothing more than a preparation. I feel as though I have done nothing yet, as though I have not lived the spiritual life, only entered the path that leads to it, it seems to me that I know nothing, that I am incapable of formulating anything, that all experience is yet to begin ..."[7]

And on 14 June Mirra wrote: "It is a veritable work of creation we have to do: to create activities, new modes of being so that this Force, unknown on earth till today, may manifest in its plenitude. To this work I am consecrated, O Lord, for this is what Thou wantest of me. But since Thou hast appointed me for this work, Thou must give me the means, that is, the knowledge necessary for its realisation ... Thou hast made a promise, Thou hast sent into these worlds those who can and that which can fulfil this promise. This now demands Thy integral help so that what has been promised may be realised. In us must take place the union of the two wills and two currents, so that from their contact may spring forth the illuminating spark. And since this *must* be done, *this will be done*."[8]

These are mysterious words which this book will have to explain. Which new modes of being were to be created? What promise was made to her by "the Lord" Himself? What was that something new that had to be realised? Radical words too, charged with a will to confront all obstacles and aware of the beginning of a new epoch in the history of humanity.

If her past had been "nothing more than a preparation", it certainly had been quite a thorough one. Mirra Richard, née Alfassa, was born in Paris in 1878, to a Turkish father and an Egyptian mother. From her earliest years she had numerous occult experiences but could not talk about them to her mother or to anybody else in the positivist milieu of her upbringings. Around the age of fifteen she began taking painting classes. This was the time of the post-impressionists and the Fauves, and she would get to know many great masters personally, among them Auguste Rodin and Henri Matisse. She would also marry

---
7. Ibid., p. 127.
8. The Mother: *Prayers and Meditations*, p. 190 (emphasis in the text).

1. An Encounter in Sleepy Pondicherry

a painter, Henri Morisset, and become an artist in her own right, and paintings of her's would be chosen for the yearly *Salon* on three successive occasions.

In 1904 Mirra discovered the *Revue Cosmique,* an occult journal directed by Max Théon and his wife, who were among the greatest occultists then alive. In this journal she found the explanations of her own occult experiences. She became its administrator. She visited the Théons twice, in 1906 and 1907, on their estate on the outskirts of Tlemcen (in Algeria), where she was instructed by them, worked together with them, and soon became at least their equal in occult knowledge and capabilities. She divorced Morisset and married Paul Richard, formerly a Protestant pastor. In those years Mirra was fairly active in all kinds of occult and spiritual circles. She befriended Alexandra David-Néel, journalist, fervent Buddhist and explorer-to-be, who would become the first Western woman to enter Lhasa, the forbidden Tibetan capital, in disguise. Mirra Richard also discovered the texts of Hinduism and Buddhism (e.g. the *Bhagavad Gita* and the *Dhammapada).* As it was her rule never to remain contented with theories but always to put them to the test, and given her natural endowments for occultism and spirituality, she made fast progress in a direction that was totally new. Later she would unexpectedly find corroboration in the spiritual explorations, discoveries and experiences of Aurobindo Ghose.

Aravinda Akroyd Ghose was born in Calcutta, in 1872, the son of a medical doctor in the service of the British colonial government and a convinced anglophile. He wanted his children to be educated according to the British model and let them speak only English and Hindustani at home; Aravinda would not learn his mother tongue until many years later. In 1879 Dr Ghose took his three young sons to England. There he entrusted their upbringing and education to a broad-minded, learned pastor in Manchester, with the strict instruction that the boys should be shielded from any contact with their motherland, its culture and its religions. Later Aravinda would study at the renowned St. Paul's School in London and at King's College in

Cambridge. While still a student, and throughout his life, he was recognised for his mastery of the English language. Also, Cambridge made him into a classical scholar. Yet he did not become what his father wanted him to be: a member of the prestigious Indian Civil Service (I.C.S.), five thousand of whom ruled over three hundred million Indians. Having gradually turned into an opponent of the British colonial regime, Aravinda deliberately failed the horse-riding test and was therefore disqualified as a candidate for the I.C.S.

In 1893 he became, apparently quite by accident, a functionary in the administration of the Maharaja of Baroda. Soon he was acting as the Maharaja's secretary and was appointed professor of English and lecturer in French at Baroda College. He was now fully involved in the study of Sanskrit, his mother tongue Bengali and other Indian languages, as well as the Indian classics. He also grew more and more involved in the freedom struggle. As soon as he was offered an opportunity Aurobindo, as he now spelled his name, left Baroda for Calcutta, the main centre of the struggle: in 1906 he was appointed Vice-Principal of the newly founded Bengal National College. The focus of his attention, however, was the daily newspaper *Bande Mataram,* which spread the message of freedom, often in Aurobindo Ghose's sonorous English, through the entire subcontinent. He was also connected with the terrorist activities of the young revolutionaries who gathered around his younger brother, Barindra.

In 1907 Aurobindo was prosecuted for his role and writings in *Bande Mataram,* but he was not convicted. By now he had become a prominent extremist leader famous all over India. The following year he was jailed and prosecuted in the Alipore Bomb Case for "treason against the Crown", a crime punishable by hanging. No sufficient proof was found against Aurobindo Ghose because a key-witness for the prosecution was killed by the revolutionaries. Aurobindo was freed, but Barindra was condemned to death and deported to the infamous jail in Port Blair on the Andaman Islands.

In the meantime a profound change had taken place in the

1. An Encounter in Sleepy Pondicherry

political extremist Aurobindo Ghose, reverent son of *Bharata Mata,* Mother India. Having seen with his own eyes that yoga could give power, and wanting power for political purposes, he called for the help of a tantric yogi. The result of this yogi's instructions was astounding, even to the instructor himself: Aurobindo achieved in a few days the realisation of the silent Brahman, something which few aspirants obtain even after a lifetime of effort. From then onwards the yoga never stopped and he followed his own path, concentrated in yoga even when intensely preoccupied with politics and journalism, and especially during his year-long incarceration in Alipore Jail. According to his own report he, like Mirra, received help from beings on the occult levels: from Ramakrishna and Vivekananda – both then deceased – and throughout from the Great Mother and Sri Krishna, who dictated to him the programme for his yogic development. Aurobindo considered Pondicherry his "cave of *tapasya*" where he worked out that programme (as shown in his diary which now is called his *Record of Yoga*) and where he continued his studies, especially of the Vedas.

Consciously unaware of the road they would tread together, Aurobindo and Mirra nevertheless had met fully prepared for such a collaboration, which the First World War would interrupt but could not terminate. In them East and West met for a new, momentous turn in the global history of humanity. If these words seem an overstatement, this book will prove otherwise. The recently published *Essays Divine and Human* show that most of what Sri Aurobindo wrote in his major works had already been experienced and realised by him before 1914. And in *Words of Long Ago* we find a note by Mirra, dated 7 May 1912, that, as she later would say, contained "the whole programme" of the work to be done, the "veritable work of creation", the establishment of "new modes of being", of a "Force unknown to the earth till today". Both of them had assimilated all that Providence had staked out for them as the nourishing ground of their experience. Both of them had thought much, still more had *seen* much and above all had experienced much.

Mirra's note reads as follows: "The general aim to be attained is the advent of a progressive universal harmony [this is what Sri Aurobindo will call 'Supermind']. The means for attaining this aim, with regard to the earth, is the realisation of human unity through the awakening in all and the manifestation by all of the inner Divinity which is One. In other words: to create unity by founding the Kingdom of God which is within us all.

"This therefore is the most useful work to be done: (1) For each, individually, to be conscious in himself of the Divine Presence and to Identify himself with it. (2) To individualise the states of being that were never till now conscious in man and, by that, to put the earth in connection with one or more of the fountains of universal force that are still sealed to it. (3) To speak again to the world the eternal word under a new form adapted to its present mentality. It will be the synthesis of all human knowledge. (4) Collectively, to establish an ideal society in a propitious spot for the flowering of the new race, the race of the Sons of God."[9]

A steep programme – which they would work out in every point, at least in principle. They lost little time and right away founded, probably at Paul Richard's prompting, the *Arya*, a "philosophical" journal intended for the exposition of their ideas. The first issue came out on Aurobindo's birthday, 15 August, a week after the outbreak of the Great War. In February of the next year the Richards were forced to leave Pondicherry. At first they went back to France and then proceeded on to Japan, where they stayed for four years. This meant that "Sri Aurobindo Ghose", as his name read on the *Arya* covers, now had to write the journal single-handed. In it he published simultaneously all his major works, with the exception of *Savitri* and a series of articles that will demand our close attention. They were written at the very end of his earthly life and are now known under the title *The Supramental Manifestation upon Earth*.

To become familiar with terms like "Supermind", and to get to the fundamentals of the matter at hand, it is necessary to sketch a brief outline of Sri Aurobindo's vision, which was Mirra's as well. For, as Sri Aurobindo wrote later, when Mirra

---

9. The Mother: *Words of Long Ago*, p. 47.

1. An Encounter in Sleepy Pondicherry

had already been the Mother of the Sri Aurobindo Ashram for several years: "There is no difference between the Mother's path and mine; we have and have always had the same path, the path that leads to the supramental change and the divine realisation; not only at the end, but from the beginning they have been the same."[10]

---

10. Sri Aurobindo: *On Himself*, p. 456.

2.
Four Pillars

Look Nature through, 'tis neat gradation all.[1]

– Edward Young (1683-1765)

Aurobindo and Mirra were from the very beginning aware of the meaning, magnitude and revolutionary portent of their joint undertaking. It was indeed, as Mirra wrote in her diary, "a veritable work of creation". To put it briefly, Aurobindo and Mirra knew that they were missioned to bring a higher consciousness onto the earth, a consciousness intended to become embodied in a new species beyond present humanity, just as the mental consciousness had embodied itself in a new species beyond the primates. It was their intention to found the Life Divine upon earth, thus fulfilling the promise made to the human species since its beginning. To put it more concretely: they intended to bring to an end the limitations and sufferings that have always been humanity's lot and turn the earth into the City of God.

They wanted, wrote Sri Aurobindo[2] in *The Life Divine,* "to search for the widest, the most flexible, the most catholic affirmation possible and found on it the largest and most comprehensive harmony."[3] "We seek indeed a larger and completer affirmation",[4] an affirmation to "square with all the facts of existence".[5] They wanted an integral knowledge to be the basis of an integral method (yoga) to transform human life into a

---
1. Quoted in Arthur Lovejoy: *The Great Chain of Being,* p. 80.
2. From here onwards in this chapter the names "Sri Aurobindo" and "Mirra" will be used, as they were printed on the cover of the *Arya.*
3. Sri Aurobindo: *The Life Divine,* p. 29.
4. Ibid., p. 24.
5. Ibid., p. 58.

2. Four Pillars

divine life on earth. "As in Science, so in metaphysical thought, that general and ultimate solution is likely to be the best which includes and accounts for all so that each truth of experience takes its place in the whole: that knowledge is likely to be the highest knowledge which illumines, integralises, harmonises the significance of all knowledge and accounts for, finds the basic and, one might almost say, the justifying reason of our ignorance and illusion while it cures them; this is the supreme experience which gathers together all experience in the truth of a supreme and all-reconciling oneness."[6]

Something similar may have been imagined or dreamed of before, but it was certainly never tried out. All expectations of a higher or a better life had always been projected into a hereafter or into an indefinite earthly future. Now, Sri Aurobindo and Mirra had acquired the conviction, based on their spiritual experience, that the time had come to realise the divine life here and now, and that it was they themselves who had to initiate the required transformation in matter, in the body, on earth. If this conception – fantastic, grandiose, utopian! – was true, then the moment of their meeting was indeed "the matrix of New Time".[7]

"We start from the idea that humanity is moving to a great change of its life which will even lead to a new life of the race,[8] – in all countries where men think, there is now in various forms that idea and that hope, – and our aim has been [in the *Arya*] to search for the spiritual, religious and other truth which can enlighten and guide the race in this movement and endeavour. *The spiritual experience and the general truths on which such an attempt could be based, were already present to us, otherwise we should have had no right to make the endeavour at all;* but the complete intellectual statement of them and their results and

---

6. Ibid., pp. 468-69.
7. Sri Aurobindo: *Savitri*, p. 399.
8. Sri Aurobindo uses the word "race" where nowadays the word "species" would be used.

issues had to be found."[9] Thus wrote Sri Aurobindo in July 1918, in an article that looked back on four years of the *Arya*.[10]

The four main pillars of Sri Aurobindo and Mirra's thought, as expounded in the *Arya*, may be summarised as follows.

1. Omnipresent Reality

"An omnipresent Reality is the truth of all life and existence whether absolute or relative, whether corporeal or incorporeal, whether animate or inanimate, whether intelligent or unintelligent; and in all its infinitely varying and even constantly opposed self-expressions, from the contradictions nearest to our ordinary experience to those remotest antinomies which lose themselves on the verges of the Ineffable, the Reality is one and not a sum or concourse. From that all variations begin, in that all variations consist, to that all variations return. All affirmations are denied only to lead to a wider affirmation of the same Reality. All antinomies confront each other in order to recognise one Truth in their opposed aspects and embrace by the way of conflict their mutual Unity. Brahman is the Alpha and the Omega. Brahman is the One besides whom there is nothing else existent."[11] That One Existent is the general experience of all mystics – those adventurers and experimenters and heroes of the spirit who had the courage to commit their lives to apparently intangible realities, and whose daring was rewarded with the direct experience of the Absolute which Indians call by that mantric word: Brahman. The Chandyoga Upanishad says it is "One without a second", and we find it in Rumi, and in Meister Eckhart who asserted that *"Gott ist eins"*, God is one.

There is, however, Brahman in its "silent" aspect: the Absolute self-existing, self-sufficient, complete in its infinity and eternity, indefinable and unnameable, as all mystics have confirmed.

---

9. Sri Aurobindo: *Essays in Philosophy and Yoga*, p. 105 (emphasis added).
10. See also by Georges Van Vrekhem: *Beyond Man – the Life and Work of Sri Aurobindo and the Mother*, and *The Mother – the Story of Her Life* (HarperCollins India).
11. Sri Aurobindo: *The Life Divine*, p. 33.

2. Four Pillars

And there is Brahman in its "active" aspect, manifesting itself in the glory of its infinite riches through all eternity – for in that Being there is neither beginning nor end. "The fundamental truth of Being must necessarily be the fundamental truth of Becoming. All is a manifestation of That."[12]

According to Indian wisdom, the three ultimate attributes of Brahman are *sat, chit* and *ananda*[13]. Existence, Consciousness and Bliss. The Absolute, That, is all-being, all-existence, all-joy. *Chit* is actually a double term, *chit-tapas* or *chit-shakti:* consciousness-force, for in the Absolute everything *seen* automatically *is*. There, there is no schism between the seeing will and its execution as there is in humans. Those three ultimate attributes are powers, powers are energies, energies are consciousnesses, consciousnesses are beings, on all levels of the manifestation. For Brahman does not create out of nothing, it manifests all out of its own being, endlessly. "Brahman is in all things, all things are in Brahman, all things are Brahman."[14]

Out of its inexhaustible riches, Brahman creates worlds without number, peopled with beings without number, all sharing in the Existence, Consciousness-Force and Joy according to their place in the universal hierarchy. For those worlds Sri Aurobindo coined the word "typal", meaning non-evolutionary; they exist outside our limitations and mortality. But among the infinite possibilities within the Absolute there was (is) the venture of the Absolute hiding himself from himself in his opposites, for reasons surpassing our understanding. And as every possibility in the Absolute must of necessity work itself out, Sachchidananda (as Sat-Chit-Ananda is spelled in one word in Anglicised Sanskrit) turned into its opposites: Being became Death, the Light of Consciousness became the Darkness of Ignorance, the Truth of Consciousness became Falsehood, Joy became Suffering. In that manner was the black Inconscient created, as infinite as its luminous Origin and containing in a covert way everything its Origin contains. In that manner was the foundation laid

---
12. Ibid., p. 660.
13. Sanskrit has no capital letters.
14. Sri Aurobindo: *The Life Divine,* p. 139.

of the adventurous development of this evolutionary world in which our souls, infinite "sparks" of the infinite Fire, chose to participate in order to experience the joy of the recovery and rediscovery of that what they – we – are and have always been: the Glory, the Ecstasy, the Divine.

2. Evolution

"Once the evolutionary hypothesis is put forward and the facts supporting it are marshalled," wrote Sri Aurobindo, "this aspect of the terrestrial existence becomes so striking as to appear indisputable."[15] Scandalously new and causing a terrible furore in the West since 1859, when Charles Darwin's *Origin of Species* was published, evolution has been part and parcel of the Hindu view of things at least since the time of the Upanishads, which in their turn point back to the Vedas.[16] "... The ancient and eternal truth of Vedanta receives into itself and illumines, justifies and shows us all the meaning of the modern and phenomenal truth of evolution in the universe. And it is so only that this modern truth of evolution which is the old truth of the Universal developing itself successively in Time, seen opaquely through the study of Force and Matter, can find its own full sense and justification, – by illuminating itself with the Light of the ancient and eternal truth still preserved for us in the Vedantic Scriptures. To this mutual self-discovery and self-illumination by the fusion of the old Eastern and the new Western knowledge the thought of the world is already turning."[17]

The clearest sources of evolutionary thinking in the Indian tradition are however to be found in the Puranas, which

---

15. Ibid., p. 836.
16. E.g. verse 1.1.8 of the Mundaka Upanishad: "Brahman grew by his energy, at work, and then from Him is Matter born, and out of Matter life, and mind and truth and the worlds, and in works immortality"; and in the Aitareya Upanishad, 1.2 verses 1 to 3, is written how man was created after the animals: "He brought unto them [the Gods] Man, and they said, 'O well fashioned truly! Man indeed is well and beautifully made'."
17. Sri Aurobindo: *The Life Divine*, p. 114.

contain the story of the succession of the Avatars. "The Hindu procession of the ten Avatars is itself, as it were, a parable of evolution."[18] An Avatar, in brief, is a direct incarnation of the Divine in his manifestation to make the next higher step in evolution possible; for the topmost established level of evolution, though driven to develop by the inherent evolutionary impulse, is unable to pierce the existing ceiling of progress. The number of Avatars varies according to the source, but generally ten Avatars are recognised. The *dasavatar* are the following: Fish, Tortoise (amphibian), Boar (mammal), Man-Lion (transitional beings between the animal kingdom and the hominids), Dwarf (first hominids), Rama-with-the-Ax (*homo habilis*), Rama-with-the-Bow, the hero of the *Ramayana* (the mental being, the human as we are), Krishna, protagonist of the *Mahabharata* (representing the Overmind, the world of the gods and religion), Buddha (shooting straight up to the indefinable Absolute) and Kalki (the future Avatar who represents Supermind). The fundamental evolutionary meaning of this "procession", theme of one of the most popular dances in the classical Indian styles, is unmistakable.

"He brought them from non-existence into being", said the great Rumi (1207-73), "from the 'pen' of being into the state of minerality, and from the pen of minerality into the state of vegetation, and from the state of vegetation into the state of animality, and from animality into the state of humanity, and from humanity into the state of angelicity, and so forth ad infinitum."[19] As Sri Aurobindo also wrote in this connection: "Another self-evident conclusion is that there is a graduated necessary succession in the evolution, first the evolution of Matter, next the evolution of Life in Matter, then the evolution of Mind in living Matter, and in this last stage an animal evolution followed by a human evolution. The first three terms of the succession are too evident to be disputable."[20] This gradation has indeed been the general way of viewing existence practically all

---

18. Sri Aurobindo: *Letters on Yoga*, p. 402.
19. Rumi: *Signs of the Unseen*, p. 21.
20. Sri Aurobindo: *The Life Divine*, p. 836.

over the world. "... [It] was [in the West that] the conception of the plan and structure of the world which, through the Middle Ages and down to the late eighteenth century ... most educated men were to accept without question – the conception of the universe as a 'Great Chain of Being,' composed of an immense, or ... infinite, number of links ranging in hierarchical order from the meagerest kind of existents ... through 'every possible' grade up to the *ens perfectissimum* [the most perfect being: the Divine]."[21] (Arthur Lovejoy)

This hierarchy of levels of existence has been brushed aside by the modern scientific-materialistic mind as magical and mystical. In the "flatland" of science only matter and nothing but matter exists. "... The triumphs of modern science went to man's head in something of the way rum does, causing him to grow loose in his logic. He came to think that what science discovers somehow casts doubt on things it does not discover; that the success it realises in its own domain throws into question the reality of domains its devices cannot touch. In short he came to assume that science implies scientism: the belief that no realities save ones that conform to the matrices science works with – space, time, matter/energy, and in the end number – exist." Thus writes Huston Smith, professor at the University of California, Berkeley, in his book *Forgotten Truth*.[22]

He is not the only scientifically knowledgeable thinker who protests so vividly against the dogmas of rigid scientism. The economist E.F. Schumacher (d. 1977), author of *Small is Beautiful*, also rediscovered the same elementary truth, which he set forth in his posthumous, often reprinted book *Guide for the Perplexed*. And there is, of course, the now widely read Ken Wilber (partly influenced by Sri Aurobindo), in whose synthetic

---

21. "... The phrase [the Great Chain of Being] ... was long one of the most famous in the vocabulary of Occidental philosophy, science, and reflective poetry; and the conception which in modern times came to be expressed by this or similar phrases has been one of the half-dozen most potent and persistent presuppositions in Western thought. It was, in fact, until not much more than a century ago, probably the most widely familiar conception of the general *scheme* of things, of the constitutive pattern of the universe ..." (Arthur Lovejoy: *The Great Chain of Being*, Preface).
22. Ibid., p. 34.

thought-frame the Great Chain of Being occupies a key position. According to him: "After being temporarily derailed in the nineteenth century by a variety of materialistic reductionisms (from scientific materialism to behaviourism to positivism), the Great Chain of Being, the Great Holarchy of Being, is making a stunning comeback."[23]

The Great Chain of Being is known under various names – "a tiered reality" (Smith), "the spectrum of consciousness" (Wilber), "the gradations of being" and "the ascending series of substance" (Sri Aurobindo) – all denoting a cosmic hierarchy of levels in which Matter would be on the lowest rung, and Spirit, or God, or the Supreme Being, on the highest. In *The Life Divine* Sri Aurobindo writes about the "sevenfold chord of Being", of which the "notes" are: matter, the vital or life-forces, mind, Supermind, Ananda, Consciousness and Being. On other occasions he mentions eight gradations. But one could also add the Inconscient and the universal subconscious below matter and the four spiritual layers of mind between the mental consciousness and Supermind (these will play an important part in our exposition further on).

One should nonetheless never lose sight of certain facts. First, that Brahman is not only at the very top of the hierarchy, but also at its very bottom and everywhere in between. Sri Aurobindo writes: "The principle of gradation we have accepted is therefore justified provided we recognise that it is one way of organising our experience and that other ways proceeding from other viewpoints are possible. For a classification can always be valid from the principle and viewpoint adopted by it while from other principles and viewpoints another classification of the same things can be equally valid."[24]

Secondly, "Consciousness is the great underlying fact"[25] everywhere in the manifestation, down from high to low and up from low to high. For Brahman *is* Consciousness, and

---

23. Ken Wilber: *The Eye of Spirit,* p. 48.
24. Sri Aurobindo: *The Life Divine,* p. 789.
25. Ibid., p. 19.

Consciousness *is* Being, and Being *is* Delight – everywhere and in everything without exception.

Thirdly, Consciousness does not evaporate as it becomes purer; on the contrary it becomes denser, more substantial, more powerful, more Being and Delight. Even the modern religious person is influenced by positivism and materialism to such a degree that everything not material is supposed to be thinner than air and therefore less and less real. Otherwise how could it be that non-material things are not subject to the laws of matter; how could they, as ghosts do, traverse matter and, as the soul supposedly does at the time of death, move about unseen and continue existing in ethereal places?

The truth, though, as re-experienced and re-affirmed by Sri Aurobindo and the Mother, is as follows: "Consciousness, as we *descend* the scale, becomes more and more diminished and diluted, – dense indeed by its coarser crudity, but while that crudity of consistence compacts the stuff of Ignorance, it admits less and less the substance of light; it becomes thin in pure substance of consciousness and reduced in power of consciousness, thin in light, thin and weak in capacity of delight; it has to resort to a grosser thickness of its diminished stuff and to a strenuous output of its obscurer force to arrive at anything, but this strenuousness of effort is a sign not of strength but of weakness. As we *ascend,* on the contrary, a finer but far stronger and more truly spiritually concrete substance emerges, a greater luminosity and potent stuff of consciousness, a subtler, sweeter, purer and more powerfully ecstatic energy of delight."[26] Therefore Sri Aurobindo, when asked what the substance of the Supermind would be, is reported to have said "lighter than a gas, denser than diamond". The understanding of the concreteness and power of the spirit in all its aspects is essential knowledge for all who want to explore it.

Putting all that together, it becomes clear that evolution in the view of Sri Aurobindo and Mirra is rather different from evolution as explained by scientific materialism. If Reality in all aspects of its manifestations, however big or small, is

---

26. Sri Aurobindo: *The Life Divine*, p. 939 (emphasis added).

always an intimate combination of the gradations mentioned above, then what really happens in the processes and stages of evolution must be something very different from any changes in matter, and much more complex. Vital, mental and supramental elements must necessarily be involved. Evolution is not only physical, it is first and foremost spiritual. "All evolution is in essence a heightening of the force of consciousness in the manifest being so that it may be raised into the greater intensity of what is still unmanifest, from matter into life, from life into mind, from mind into the spirit."[27]

Sri Aurobindo wrote even more explicitly: "A theory of spiritual evolution is not identical with a scientific theory of form-evolution and physical life-evolution; it must stand on its own inherent justification: it may accept the scientific account of physical evolution as a support or an element, but *the support is not indispensable*. The scientific theory is concerned only with the outward and visible machinery and process, with the detail of Nature's execution, with the physical development of things in Matter and the law of development of Life and Mind in Matter; its account of the process may have to be considerably changed [as in the meantime it has on several occasions] or may be dropped altogether in the light of a new discovery, but that will not affect the self-evident fact of a spiritual evolution, an evolution of Consciousness, a progression of the soul's manifestation in material existence."[28]

There is, finally, an important concept to be found in the scheme of things as proposed by Sri Aurobindo and Mirra: the concept of involution. Involution, it goes without saying, is the opposite of evolution. As Sri Aurobindo puts it: "Evolution is an inverse action of the involution."[29] Logic as well as spiritual experience made it clear to him that nothing can evolve which has not previously been involved. The fact of universal evolution is naturally the consequence of the Divine "hiding himself from himself" as mentioned earlier. "This descent of

---
27. Sri Aurobindo: *The Life Divine*, p. 726.
28. Ibid., p. 836 (emphasis added).
29. Ibid., p. 853.

"the supreme Reality is in its nature a self-concealing", writes Sri Aurobindo, "and in the descent there are successive levels, in the concealing successive veils. Necessarily, the revelation takes the form of an ascent; and necessarily also the ascent and the revelation are both progressive" – which summarises the process of involution and evolution. "We have to conceive first of an involution and a self-absorption of conscious being into the density and infinite divisibility of substance, for otherwise there can be no finite variation. Next, an emergence of the self-imprisoned force into formal [material] being, living being, thinking being; and finally a release of the formed thinking being into the free realisation of itself as the One and the Infinite at play in the world and by the release its recovery of the boundless existence-consciousness-bliss that even now it is secretly, really and eternally. This triple movement is the whole key of the world-enigma."[30]

3. Supermind

The most obvious gradations of being are the ones that play a directly perceptible role in the constitution of our being and our life: matter, the vital (life-forces) and the mental (rational consciousness). These are therefore the gradations rediscovered and revalued by nonconformist thinkers like E.F. Schumacher and Huston Smith. Yet, as we have seen, the stair of being goes all the way upwards from the Inconscient to the Supreme (as first it has gone all the way downwards).

Looking up from our position on material Mother Earth towards the "heavens" with their hierarchical regions of invisible beings, and normally lacking any conscious connection with those higher worlds, we feel there is a gap between the two realms, between the higher and lower hemispheres of global existence. The very concrete experience of this gap is at the basis of spiritual paths like Buddhism and Advaita, as it is the cause of the Western view which puts God, the angels and

---

30. Sri Aurobindo: *The Life Divine*, pp. 113-14.

the saints in heaven, and suffering humanity on earth, in "the valley of tears". According to the first view the world is unreal, according to the second view it is worthless and inexplicable. The principal aim of both kinds of spiritual or religious endeavour, in both East and West, consists in escaping as quickly as possible from the absurd ordeal of earthly embodiment into the promised (but not proven) relief of a hereafter.

As we will see further on, the thought of Sri Aurobindo and Mirra, based on their extensively tested spiritual experience, goes radically against such long established views. If all is That, the Brahman or Absolute, then there is no gainsaying that matter and the earth too must be That. They must have a divine meaning because they have a divine essence, for they cannot but be composed of the Divine in its essential attributes of Being, Consciousness-Force and Bliss. This radical reversal by Sri Aurobindo and Mirra of the essential values, declaring the world "worthy"[31], was based on a spiritual discovery whose time seemed to have come: Supermind, the link between God in his heaven and the human being on his planet.

Mirra as well as Sri Aurobindo had come into contact with "an intermediate link between the two [hemispheres] which can explain them to each other and establish between them such a relation as will make it possible for us to realise the one Existence, Consciousness, Delight in the mould of the mind, life and body. The intermediate link exists. We call it the Supermind or the Truth-Consciousness, because it is a principle superior to mentality and exists, acts and proceeds in the fundamental truth and unity of things and not like the mind in their appearances and phenomenal divisions."[32] It was this discovery, this inner experience and knowledge, that Mirra brought with her when she met Sri Aurobindo and discovered that he had the same realisation. In the West as well as in the East, at the same time, a new light had begun to dawn.

To us, ordinary mortals, Supermind is a mere word. Neither

---

31. *Worthy is the World* is the title of a book by Beatrice Bruteau on Sri Aurobindo's philosophy (Fairleigh Dickinson University Press).
32. Sri Aurobindo: *The Life Divine*, p. 143.

Mirra nor Sri Aurobindo were very happy with it. "The word is ambiguous", wrote Sri Aurobindo, its coiner, "since it may be taken in the sense of mind itself, super-eminent and lifted above ordinary mentality but not radically changed, or on the contrary it may bear the sense of all that is beyond mind and therefore assume a too extensive comprehensiveness which would bring in even the Ineffable [the Supreme] itself."[33]

Then what is Supermind? Brahman need not manifest itself, it is perfect in its absoluteness and not dependent on any manifestation. If it were dependent on manifestation, it would not be Brahman. Yet for reasons unknowable to beings with a consciousness like ours and which in India are called its *lila*[34], its play, Brahman does manifest. This manifesting power or part of Brahman is called "Supermind" by its discoverers, Sri Aurobindo and Mirra. It should be added at once that this manifesting part or power is nothing subordinate to the Absolute. No part of the Divine is subordinate to the whole – not even our own soul. All parts of the Divine are fully divine, just as all parts of the infinite are infinite. Supermind belongs to the upper hemisphere, together with the Being, Consciousness and Bliss. Again: these are not abstractions but realities, infinite realms of divine glory far beyond our understanding and imagination. As is Supermind.

"We have to regard therefore this all-containing, all-originating, all-consummating Supermind as the nature of the Divine Being, not indeed in its absolute self-existence, but in its action as the Lord and Creator of its own worlds. This is the truth of that which we call God. Obviously this is not the too personal and limited Deity, the magnified and supernatural Man of the ordinary occidental conception; for that conception erects a too human eidolon of a certain relation between the creative Supermind and the ego."[35]

---

33. Ibid., p. 124.
34. "All exists here, no doubt, for the delight of existence, all is a game or Lila; but a game too carries within itself an object to be accomplished and without the fulfilment of that object would have no completeness or significance." Sri Aurobindo: *The Life Divine,* p. 835.
35. Sri Aurobindo: *The Life Divine,* p. 132.

2. Four Pillars

Supermind is a Unity-Consciousness, totally and effectively aware of everything, omniscient. Supermind is a Truth-Consciousness containing all existence in a perfect relation of harmony and therefore omnipotent – for, remember, what the Divine sees in itself *is*. "Supramental nature sees everything from the standpoint of oneness and regards all things, even the greatest multiplicity and diversity, even what are to the mind the strongest contradictions, in the light of the oneness; its will, ideas, feelings, sense are made of the stuff of oneness, its actions proceed upon that basis. Mental nature, on the contrary, thinks, sees, wills, feels, senses with division as a starting-point and has only a constructed understanding of unity; even when it experiences oneness, it has to act from the oneness on a basis of limitation and difference. But the supramental, the divine life is a life of essential, spontaneous and inherent unity."[36]

As all is in all, Supermind was present in the manifestation since its inception. It caused the manifestation – the typal worlds and our evolutionary world – to be and supports them in every detail, for without it they would collapse into non-existence. "This Supermind in its conscious vision not only contains all the forms of itself which its conscious force creates, but it pervades them as an indwelling Presence and a self-revealing Light", writes Sri Aurobindo. "It is present, even though concealed, in every form and force of the universe ... It is seated within everything as the Lord in the heart of all existences, – he who turns them as on an engine by the power of his Maya; it is within them and embraces them as the divine Seer who variously disposed and ordained objects, each rightly according to the thing that it is, from years sempiternal. Each thing in Nature, therefore, whether animate or inanimate, mentally self-conscious or not self-conscious, is governed in its being and in its operation by an indwelling Vision and Power, to us subconscient or inconscient because we are not conscious of it, but not inconscient to itself, rather profoundly and universally conscient."[37]

---

36. Ibid., p. 965.
37. Sri Aurobindo: *The Life Divine*, p. 135.

A text like this touches upon the fantastic complexity of matter, able to combine itself in functional clusters, from an atom to a galaxy and with all that there is in between. "Something", far beyond our imagination, must be directing that show. Confiding the whirling universe to Chance actually demonstrates a greater power of belief than confiding it to a Consciousness. The problem lies in the fact that generally speaking the Western mind still has such a childish idea of "God". It studies the different theorems of science, but refuses to study the difficult approaches to "God". This is, however, understandable, for in this it has been misled and cheated so often.

The crucial importance of the discovery of Supermind lies in the fact that Sri Aurobindo and Mirra were convinced that this concealed Consciousness now had to become active as the next stage in the earthly evolution, which means that it would be embodied on the earth in a new species of beings. This Consciousness being divine, the new beings would also be divine. "For Supermind is Superman."[38] As the physical aspects of evolution are the results of an evolution of consciousness, every important evolutionary step depends on two factors. On the one hand there is the unstoppable evolutionary impulse or "nisus" (a word often used by Sri Aurobindo) pushing up from below; on the other hand there is the new consciousness answering, descending from above. For, as noted before, the manifestation encompasses all levels of consciousness in a "stair", a graded hierarchy of typal worlds. Those levels of consciousness, those worlds, are the evolutionary scale of our world inserted as it were one after the other, hierarchically. After the "miracle" of the phenomena of matter emerging from the Inconscient, there was the "miracle" of the vegetal and animal life-forms taking shape in lifeless matter, followed by the "miracle" of a rationally conscious *homo sapiens*. Seen like this, a new evolutionary miracle would be a rather logical occurrence.

"The advance [towards supermanhood], however it comes about, will be indeed of the nature of a miracle", wrote Sri Aurobindo, "as are all such profound changes and immense

---
38. Ibid., p. 44.

development; for they have the appearance of a kind of realised impossibility. But God works all his miracles by an evolution of secret possibilities which have been long prepared, at least in their elements, and in the end by a rapid bringing of all to a head, a throwing together of the elements so that in their fusion they produce a new form and name of things and reveal a new spirit. Often the decisive turn is preceded by an apparent emphasising and raising to their extreme of things which seem the very denial, the most uncompromising opposite of the new principle and the new creation."[39]

In short, if evolution has a meaning, and if it is the Supreme himself who is evolving in the evolution, then it seems incredible that he would not be able to produce something better than the species that considers itself the top of creation. "This ignorant, imperfect and divided being, with his labouring uncertain thought and half-successful will, this toiling and fluctuating experiment, this field of the attempt at emergence of a thousand things that are striving to be, is no consummation of the struggle of cosmic Force; he is only a laboratory in which Nature seeks for its own concealed secret, makes tentative efforts at what she has been missioned to achieve. As man arose out of the animal, so out of man superman shall come."[40]

The superman has always been living in humanity's dreams of power, invulnerability, immortality, boundless knowledge, omnipresence, and of a love permanently as exhilarating and pure as first love. If the longing to fly is there, it may be realised one day in a much simpler and smoother way than airplanes do today. If the longing to talk and see at a distance is there, it may be realised without the complicated and fragile machines needed at present. And those people who have long laboured to acquire a certain knowledge, and are therefore called sages, say that the abiding and ever enraptured love is already present in that dimensionless being hidden behind our heart, and that it can become a constant, conscious state that never turns sour. We – our species – will have to find that out. "It is impossible

---
39. Sri Aurobindo: *The Human Cycle*, p. 183.
40. Sri Aurobindo: *Essays Divine and Human*, p. 26.

for the mind to forecast in detail what the supramental change must be in its parts of life-action and outward behaviour or lay down for it what forms it shall create for the individual or the collective existence. For the mind acts by intellectual rule or device or by reasoned choice of will or by mental impulse or in obedience to the life-impulse; but supramental nature does not act by mental idea or rule or in subjection to any inferior impulse: each of its steps is dictated by an innate spiritual vision, a comprehensive and exact penetration into the truth of all and the truth of each thing; it acts always according to inherent reality, not by the mental idea, not according to an imposed law of conduct or a constructive thought or perceptive contrivance."[41]

"We are in respect to our possible higher evolution much in the position of the original Ape of the Darwinian theory", writes Sri Aurobindo in *The Life Divine*. "It would have been impossible for that Ape leading his instinctive arboreal life in primeval forests to conceive that there would be one day an animal on the earth who would use a new faculty called reason upon the materials of his inner and outer existence, who would dominate by that power his instincts and habits, change the circumstances of his physical life, build for himself houses of stone, manipulate Nature's forces, sail the seas, ride the air, develop codes of conduct, evolve conscious methods for his mental and spiritual development. Man, because he has acquired reason and still more because he has indulged his power of imagination and intuition, is able to conceive an existence higher than his own and even to envisage his personal elevation beyond his present state into that existence. His idea of the supreme state is an absolute of all that is positive to his own concepts and desirable to his own instinctive aspiration ... It is so that he conceives his gods; it is so that he constructs his heavens. But it is not so that his reason conceives of the possible earth and a possible humanity. His dream of God and Heaven is really a dream of his own perfection; but he finds the same difficulty in accepting its practical realisation here for

---

41. Sri Aurobindo: *The Life Divine*, p. 965.

his ultimate aim as would the ancestral Ape if called upon to believe in himself as the future Man."[42]

A last reflection on the subject of superman: no sooner have most people heard the word "superman" pronounced than they associate it with the ideas of Friedrich Nietzsche (d. 1900). Sri Aurobindo knew the writings of that "half-luminous Hellenising Slav", the "apostle who never entirely understood his own message",[43] much better than is commonly supposed. He even appreciated him to a certain degree. "Nietzsche's idea that to develop the superman out of our present very unsatisfactory manhood is our real business, is in itself an absolutely sound teaching. His formulation of our aim, 'to become ourselves', 'to exceed ourselves', implying, as it does, that man has not yet found his true self, his true nature by which he can successfully and spontaneously live, could not be bettered. But then the question of questions is there, what is our self, and what is our real nature? What is that which is growing in us, but into which we have not yet grown?"[44] The gist of Sri Aurobindo's answers to these questions has been given in the previous pages. To the person who has read them and who has some inkling of Nietzsche's thinking it should be clear that there is a world of difference between the two ideals of the superman.

4. At the Crossroads of Evolution: "homo sapiens"

Much, if not most, of the confusion in Western philosophy and psychology, and in Western thinking in general, is caused by the defective, distorted image the West has of the human being. The distortion was symptomatic in the doctrine of Christianity, and the materialistic dogma of scientism, which abandoned the world-view of the Great Chain of Being for what Ken Wilber calls "flatland", has made it worse.

The authentic occult traditions, Hermetism for instance,

---
42. Ibid., pp. 55-56.
43. Sri Aurobindo: *Essays in Philosophy and Yoga*, p. 151.
44. Sri Aurobindo: *The Human Cycle*, p. 233.

knew a lot more about the human being than either Christianity or modern Science. The simple reason is that their knowledge was based on occult or spiritual experience.[45] They also had a far higher opinion of humankind, putting it often above the gods, and always saw the human being as a *microcosm,* the cosmos in miniature, containing or at least reflecting in itself everything the cosmos contains. The Indian traditions confirm the same insight, and Sri Aurobindo and Mirra, who sometimes referred to a tradition "older than the Veda and the Chaldean tradition", frequently spoke or wrote about "man, the microcosm". "All things are potentially contained in that substance that constitutes man ... In an essential way, each being contains in itself all the universal potentialities."[46]

Let us briefly sketch a picture of the self-ignorant wonder that is the human being. Just like the rest of the cosmos it is composed of the gradations of existence that have so far evolved: material, vital and mental. Sri Aurobindo often stressed that the human being is specifically the mental being, the typical embodiment of the mental gradation of the universal manifestation. "The mind pre-eminently is man; he is a mental being and his human perfection grows the more he fulfils the description of the Upanishad, a mental being, Purusha, leader of the life and the body."[47] Not only are there in the human these three very apparent elements, there is also a soul, a "divine spark", which is the cause and support of the triple-layered bodily existence.

Above the rational consciousness there are, moreover, levels of the spiritual consciousness, which we will consider in detail in a subsequent chapter. It is from these levels that humanity gets the fine flower of its intuitions and inspirations; it is from there that it gets its first glimpses of enlightenment; it is through these levels that the great ideas, the great essences descend that shape and change the world. The advanced in

---

45. "Occult" is what is invisible, "spiritual" is what belongs to the realms above our rational consciousness. Therefore all that is spiritual is necessarily occult, but all that is occult is not necessarily spiritual – far from it, for it may belong to or emanate from realms much lower than rational consciousness.
46. The Mother: *Questions and Answers* 1955, p. 387.
47. Sri Aurobindo: *Essays in Philosophy and Yoga*, p. 530.

Spirit have access to those suprarational levels (which are still far below "Supermind").

Below matter there is also, as we know, the Inconscient, out of which this evolutionary cosmos has arisen in the course of eons. Actually, it was only when something in the Inconscient itself had evolved and become what Sri Aurobindo and Mirra call the "subconscious" that matter could be formed and evolution take a physical shape. Both these levels of darkness the human being also carries in himself, they cause "the downward gravitation" in him which counteracts every upward effort. They are pure hell, the locus of the impulses that incite the killer and the sadist. They are the constant presence behind all horrors and evil.

Then there is what Sri Aurobindo termed the "subliminal" which constitutes a sort of aura through which other worlds and beings contact and influence us. We are actually constantly surrounded by hundreds of invisible beings of all kinds, by thousands of free floating vital entities, and by clouds of thoughts or shreds of thoughts, some of which gain entrance into our head and are then deemed our own. In fact, a truly personal thought is a rare phenomenon, and so is a truly personal feeling.

All this makes the human being into an extremely complex entity. This complexity is one of the reasons why so few people know themselves, and why their personality consists of many compartments to which their active consciousness has no access. The ordinary human is for the most part ignorant (and indignant when told so), and does not master much of the terrain that is his or her very own dominion.

If all this may seem somewhat abstract or "occult", the direct effects of the gradations of being on our body and life are very concrete. Firstly, there are the *chakras* (literally "wheels"), the energy centres in our subtle body which are the gates, as it were, to the universal gradations and forces of being. Normally these centres are almost fully closed, thus protecting us from the inrush of the stupendous cosmic powers for which the human capacities of resistance and mastery are no match. Normally, these chakras can only be opened by a long and patient yogic discipline under the supervision of a qualified guru.

At the bottom of the spine there is the chakra containing the *kundalini*, the "serpent power", the direct connection with the universal force of materialisation and therefore the cornerstone of our bodily incarnation. Higher up are three vital chakras, the lowest being the sex centre, then the navel centre commanding vital feelings like anger, fear and greed, while the higher vital feelings (courage, generosity, sympathy and "love") are dependent on the heart centre. This centre has a double function, for if opened, it also gives access to the soul, whose locus in the human material embodiment is just behind the heart. (This double function is the reason why the emotions and the soul are so often confused and intermingled.) Still higher up there are the three mental chakras: mental expression and communication in the throat, mental concentration and formation between and slightly above the eyes (the "third eye"), and "the thousand-petalled lotus" of the higher mental levels just above the head and touching its crown.

Humanity being what it is at present, the centre above the head does duty for all that is as yet supramental. If other suprarational layers of consciousness grew functional for earthly beings, then higher centres above the head would become active. The Mother has reported this from her own experience. She also said, in a conversation in 1954,[48] that there are not seven but twelve chakras. This is understandable in the light of what precedes, for the subconscious and the Inconscient, which play such an important role in the life of the human being, certainly must have their own chakra below that of the kundalini. Likewise the levels of Overmind and Supermind must have their physical contact points with a materially incarnated being once they have become actively conscious in that being.

Another direct effect of the gradations of being are the multiple bodies or "sheaths" into which our soul has incarnated. There is not only the most obvious sheath, the material body, there is also a vital and a mental sheath (and potentially a

---

48. See the Mother: *Questions and Answers*, p. 77.

2. Four Pillars

"causal" or supramental one). These bodies together form what Indians call the *adhara*. This is the reason why, when we leave our material body (in our dreams or when we die), we still exist and move about in our vital and mental bodies. It is the sojourn after death in the vital body, which then has to pass through kindred vital worlds, that is the origin of the belief in "hell", for the lower vital worlds and the beings dwelling in those worlds can truly be infernal. When the vital body too is discarded, the soul still has to pass through mental worlds before it can enter the soul world, where it then assimilates the experiences of the past life and prepares for the next one.

This view of the human being is at loggerheads with the view materialistic science holds up to us. It is, however, much closer to the facts of human experience and can help us to gain a true understanding of the enigma that we are to ourselves. We are now ready for a look at the position of *homo sapiens* in evolution. The following quotations from Sri Aurobindo need no comment.

"This evolution, it is sometimes pretended, ends in man, man is the term and end; but this is because we miss the real values of the process. At first indeed we see this Spirit spending numberless millions of years to evolve a material system of worlds empty of life in the beginning, a lesser but vast enough series of millions to develop an earth on which life can inhabit, a lesser series of millions to make possible and train, raise life itself with but a feeble and restricted apparatus of mind; but once it has found a body, a brain, a living apparatus not perfect, but still sufficient, it is no longer concerned mainly with evolving a body or ... [49] an embodied life can but at last grapple with its own proper business. Evolution henceforth means the evolution of the consciousness, of mind and, if any such thing there be, of what is beyond mind, – and in that case as its last stride has been the evolution of the mental being, man, out of the

---

49. This text is a handwritten note by Sri Aurobindo from the years before the *Arya*. The ellipse indicates an indecipherable word.

vital being, the animal, so its next stride will be to evolve out of mental man a greater spiritual and supramental creature."[50]

"Man is an abnormal who has not found his own normality, – he may imagine he has, he may appear to be normal in his own kind, but that normality is only a sort of provisional order; therefore, though man is infinitely greater than the plant or the animal, he is not perfect in his own nature like the plant and the animal. This imperfection is not a thing to be at all deplored, but rather a privilege and a promise, for it opens out to us an immense vista of self-development and self-exceeding. Man at his highest is a half-god who has risen up out of the animal Nature and is splendidly abnormal in it, but the thing which he has started out to be, the whole god, is something so much greater than what he is that it seems to him as abnormal to himself as he is to the animal."[51]

"If a spiritual unfolding on earth is the hidden truth of our birth into Matter, if it is fundamentally an evolution of consciousness that has been taking place in Nature, then man as he is cannot be the last term of that evolution: He is too imperfect an expression of the Spirit, Mind itself is a too limited form and instrumentation; Mind is only a middle term of consciousness, the mental being can only be a transitional being. If, then, man is incapable of exceeding mentality, he must be surpassed and Supermind and superman must manifest and take the lead of the creation. But if his mind is capable of opening to what exceeds it, then there is no reason why man himself should not arrive at Supermind and supermanhood or *at least lend his mentality, life and body to an evolution of that greater term of the spirit manifesting in Nature.*"[52]

"This is the meaning of our existence here, its futuristic value and inherent trend of power, to rise above ourselves, to grow into gods, to reveal God in a world of material forms and forces. Earth and conscious life upon earth are not a freak of cosmic Chance, a meaningless accident in the vacant history

---

50. Sri Aurobindo: *Essays Divine and Human*, p. 223.
51. Sri Aurobindo: *The Human Cycle*, p. 234.
52. Sri Aurobindo: *The Life Divine*, p. 847 (emphasis added).

of nebula and electron and gas and plasm; they are the field of a game of the Gods with the destiny of our souls as the stake of their wager. To evolve Godhead out of the mud of matter, some divinest consciousness out of a primal inconscience and a struggling ignorance, immortality out of death, undying bliss out of pain and sorrow, the everlasting Truth out of the falsehoods and denials of this relative world is their great and daring gamble."[53]

And lastly: "The animal is man in the making; man himself is that animal and yet the something more of self-consciousness and dynamic power of consciousness that make him man; and yet again he is the something more which is contained and repressed in his being as the potentiality of the divine, – he is a god in the making. In each of these, plant, animal, man, god, the Eternal is there containing and repressing himself as it were in order to make a certain statement of his being. Each is the whole Eternal concealed. Man himself, who takes up all that went before him and transmutes it into the term of manhood, is the individual human being and yet he is all mankind, the universal man acting in the individual as a human personality. He is all and yet he is himself and unique. He is what he is, but he is also the past of all that he was and the potentiality of all that he is not. We cannot understand him if we look only at his present individuality ..."[54]

---

53. Sri Aurobindo: *Essays Divine and Human*, p. 261.
54. Sri Aurobindo: *The Life Divine*, pp. 381-82.

3.
Turning Towards the Earth

Our father Heaven must remain bright with the hope of deliverance, but also our mother Earth must not feel herself for ever accursed.[1]

– Sri Aurobindo

The contents of the previous chapter may seem unusual, bizarre, esoteric, or simply outlandish to a mind conditioned by the present-day Western "consensus reality". But once the premises of an omnipresent Reality and an evolutionary development of the successive degrees of existence are accepted, the conclusions as drawn by Sri Aurobindo and Mirra are perfectly logical. This is why Sri Aurobindo himself characterised their view of things as "a rational and philosophic truth which is in accordance with all the rest we have hitherto known, experienced, or been able to think out about the overt truth of our existence."[2] If evolution is true, then it is only the time it takes before a radical change in the existing situation happens – i.e. before a new species appears on the scene – that has accustomed us to the idea that we humans are on the top rung of the ladder of life on earth, and will remain there for as long as there will be life on this planet.

When might such a radical change in the existing situation happen? If it happens in a million or several million years from now, then we, living under the threat of a nuclear holocaust, will be hardly interested – especially now, when the exploding human population on the planet seems to have lost its bearings and nothing makes sense to us anymore, except the instant

---
1. Sri Aurobindo: *The Upanishads,* p. 188.
2. Sri Aurobindo: *The Life Divine,* p. 260.

gratification of our desires. Sri Aurobindo and Mirra, however, were convinced that the evolutionary experiment on this planet would run its full course, and that the mutation into a new species was to be initiated now. Indeed, they believed themselves missioned to set the process going, to take the first basic, transformative steps and secure the transition into a new world.

They were not naïve, for their life experience, their insight into human nature and their spiritual explorations had been too thorough for that. And although they may have underestimated the difficulty of some aspects of the enormously complex process of transformation, they were nevertheless aware of the huge scale of the task they were taking upon their shoulders. We must remember that this task consisted in opening the lower hemisphere of existence to the higher, in bringing Light and Knowledge where now there is darkness and ignorance, in changing the human life into "the life divine". If ever there was a change or crisis in humanity, then the present one certainly must be greater than any other in the past. And if a profound crisis in the development of humanity requires a direct embodiment of the Divine in its manifestation, in other words an Avatar, then this very profound crisis certainly required the descent of an Avatar, the Avatar of the Supermind. But this time the Avatar came not in a single, male body as on all previous occasions: he came as a complete incarnation of the male and female poles of existence in Sri Aurobindo and Mirra.

Once again, does this sound too unusual, bizarre, esoteric or outlandish? The established religions tell us that everything worthwhile in religion has happened in the past, and nothing of fundamental religious importance can happen in times like ours. "The traditions of the past are very great in their own place, in the past," wrote Sri Aurobindo trenchantly, "but I do not see why we should merely repeat them and not go farther. In the spiritual development of the consciousness upon earth the great past ought to be followed by a great future."[3] This does not sound unreasonable. And is the century that just ended not suggestive of a change never before witnessed in the history of

---
3. Sri Aurobindo: *On Himself*, p. 122.

humanity? If the signs are there, the facts and their cause may be there too. But seldom have humans been aware of a vital change in their way of being, at the moment the change came to pass, even the ones who were instrumental in their own revolutions.

"Matter also is Brahman"

If everything is Brahman, then, of course, matter too is Brahman, even the gross kind of matter held by scientific materialism to be the only one existent, while in fact it is but one of the many gradations of substance which lend concreteness to the tiers of being. For vital beings exist in vital substance, mental beings in mental substance, supramental beings in supramental substance. "[Matter] is a fit and noble material out of which He weaves constantly His garbs, builds recurrently the unending series of His mansions."[4] The Upanishads describe the physical universe of gross matter "as the external body of the Divine Being".[5] Therefore matter, arisen from the Inconscient – Sri Aurobindo described our body as "a flower of the material Inconscience" – is "a form of the Spirit, a habitation of the Spirit, and here in Matter itself there can be a realisation of the Spirit".[6]

If a higher, more refined species of being is to appear in a world of gross matter, then the grossness has to be refined. It is because this alchemic work of transformation has to take place in earthly matter that Sri Aurobindo gave so much importance to the essential divinity and transformability of this kind of substance. The earth seems after all to be a much more special cosmic body than is postulated in the current cosmological model. "Our attention must be fixed on the earth because our work is here. Besides, the earth is a concentration of all the other worlds and one can touch them by touching something

---
4. Sri Aurobindo: *On Himself,* p. 373.
5. Ibid.
6. Ibid., p. 665.

corresponding in the earth-atmosphere",[7] wrote Sri Aurobindo. And the Mother said: "The earth is a kind of symbolic crystallisation of universal life, a reduction, a concentration, so that the work of evolution may be easier to do and follow. And if we see the history of the earth, we can understand why the universe has been created. It is the Supreme growing aware of himself in an eternal Becoming; and the goal is the union of the created with the Creator, a union that is conscious, willing and free, in the Manifestation."[8] The earth, in their view, was once more elevated, not physically but symbolically, to a central place in the universe and its evolution. The earth was again considered a living being, the Earth Mother, whose children we literally are.

"However high we may climb, even though it be to the Non-Being itself, we climb ill if we forget our base",[9] wrote Sri Aurobindo in the *Arya*. Even a casual survey of the world's chief religions will show how innovative a standpoint this was at the beginning of the twentieth century. As noted, all major religions condemn the world as a place of suffering, and no religion has a rationally adequate explanation for our being here and having to undergo the ordeal. There are stories, there are myths telling in most cases about a coincidence or accident that caused us to get lost here, but none of those tales offers a convincing rationale. The reasons for escape from life as systematised by Buddhism, for instance, or by Advaitic Illusionism are much more convincing. In fact these religions, with India as their centre of propagation, have convinced and converted whole peoples.

Sri Aurobindo and Mirra took an outspoken stance against what the latter called a "supreme act of egoism" that escapism from the world and from life in all its aspects is. "Buddha and Shankara supposed the world to be radically false and miserable; therefore escape from the world was to them the only wisdom. But this world is Brahman, the world is God, the world is Satyam, the world is Ananda; it is our misreading of

---

7. Sri Aurobindo: *On the Mother*, p. 373.
8. The Mother: *Questions and Answers 1957-58*, p. 320.
9. Sri Aurobindo: *The Life Divine*, p. 36.

the world through mental egoism that is a falsehood and our wrong relation with God in the world that is a misery. There is no other falsity and no other cause of sorrow."[10]

This is the reason why an important part of *The Life Divine* is actually an argumentation against Buddhism and Advaitic Illusionism. They are, according to Sri Aurobindo, responsible for India's deterioration because of their exclusive concentration on "the other world". He esteemed Gautama the Buddha (563-483 BC) as gifted with a "penetrating rational intellect supported by an intuitive vision",[11] and called Adi Shankara (788-820 AD) "easily the first of metaphysical thinkers, the greatest genius in the history of philosophy". All the same, "it remains true that Shankara's commentary is interesting not so much for the light it sheds on the Upanishad as for its digressions into his own philosophy ... The time is fast coming when the human intellect, aware of the mighty complexity of the universe, will be more ready to learn and less prone to dispute and dictate; we shall be willing then to read ancient documents of knowledge for what they contain instead of attempting to force into them our own truth or get them to serve our philosophic or scholastic purposes."[12]

Sri Aurobindo was "concerned with the earth" and so, of course, was Mirra. Already before meeting Sri Aurobindo she had written in her diary: "Even he who might have attained a perfect contemplation in silence and solitude would have

---

10. Sri Aurobindo: *Essays Divine and Human*, p. 96. "Generally speaking, individual salvation has been the highest aim of spiritual seeking in our country. For in pluralism the souls are entirely distinct from one another, whereas for monism, which considers the soul to be nothing but the absolute Spirit, the soul's perception of other individuals is an illusion. Therefore in both cases liberation is only an individual issue. Further, they insist that since embodied life is due to an inexplicable fall of the soul into Matter, liberation is not only freedom from false identification with the body but complete withdrawal from embodied life as well. But for Sri Aurobindo individual liberation is not an end in itself, but only a means to emancipate the divine consciousness in the collective existence and establish a divine life upon earth." N. Jayashanmugam: *Veda and Vedanta: New Interpretations*, p. 40.
11. Ibid., p. 464.
12. Sri Aurobindo: *The Upanishads*, p. 334.

arrived at it only by withdrawing from his body, by disregarding it, and so the substance of which the body is constituted would remain as impure, as imperfect as before, since he would have left it to itself; and by a misguided mysticism, through the lure of supraphysical splendours, the egoistic desire to unite with Thee for his own personal satisfaction, he would have turned his back upon the very reason of his earthly existence, he would have cowardly refused to accomplish his mission of redemption, of purification of Matter. To know that a part of our being is perfectly pure, to commune with this purity, to be identified with it, can be useful only if this knowledge is later used to hasten the earthly transfiguration, to accomplish Thy sublime work."[13] (This is strong evidence that Mirra and Sri Aurobindo's paths were the same from the beginning.)

The Radical Spirit

Nowadays it is often forgotten how novel and daring, how uncompromising was Sri Aurobindo and the Mother's enterprise when they took it up. When reading them, one may become satiated with reading about superman, Supermind, a divine body and paradise upon earth. But if concrete results are not forthcoming and life keeps passing by without any experience of the things promised, then what was at first a revelation becomes little by little no more than an inspiring fiction, and the great literature in which the revelation is packed covers the contents. The results, however, *are there* – this is what this book is all about – and it is therefore important to recall, at least in passing, the radical spirit in which Sri Aurobindo and the Mother took up their heavy task and worked it out every minute of their existence. And they always expressed themselves very clearly and, at times, forcefully.

The quiet, gentlemanly Aurobindo Ghose had always been a radical. His series of political articles "New Lamps for Old", written in 1893 when he was twenty-one, was terminated by the

---

13. The Mother: *Prayers and Meditations*, p. 20.

editor of the *Indu Prakash* because the articles where so scathing that the editor feared the colonial rulers might take offence. We know already that Aurobindo staked his life on achieving the freedom of his Motherland. What is not well known is that he was the very first to demand unconditional freedom for India. Later he would write about himself in the third person: "He always stood for India's complete independence which he was the first to advocate publicly without compromise as the only ideal worthy of a self-respecting nation"; and on another occasion: "Sri Aurobindo's first preoccupation was to declare openly for complete and absolute independence as the aim of political action in India and to insist on this persistently in the pages of the journal [*Bande Mataram*]; he was the first politician in India who had the courage to do this in public ..."[14] He withdrew from politics only when he was sure that the idea of unconditional freedom was firmly imprinted on the political mind of India and that its eventual realisation was assured.

Mirra's life was not less radical. She had to break with her bourgeois background to enter the "bohemian" life of the artists' world in Paris. The risks she took in her occult explorations were considerable, and once she actually died for a short time because her own teacher, in a fit of anger, cut the silver cord connecting the subtle sheaths with the material body. (The combined knowledge of herself and of her teacher succeeded in bringing her painfully back to life.) The battle with the hostile being incarnated in her second husband must have been frightful, but we get only scarce glimpses of it. What are most extensively documented are her risky adventures later in life, after 1958, when she took up the transformation of her physical body.

"My whole life has been a struggle with hard realities", wrote Sri Aurobindo in a letter meant to put the record straight, "from hardships, starvation in England and constant dangers and fierce difficulties to the far greater difficulties continually cropping up here in Pondicherry, external and internal. My life has been a battle from its early years and is still a battle: the fact

---

14. Sri Aurobindo: *On Himself,* p. 29.

that I wage it now from a room upstairs and by spiritual means as well as others that are external makes no difference to its character."[15]

Two remarks may put the above into the correct perspective. Firstly, the "hostile beings" were very real to Sri Aurobindo and the Mother. They belong mainly to the vital worlds, but also partially to mental worlds, and are dominating the earth in its present state. This dominion they want to keep, and as their nature is sheer ego, their methods and actions are ruthless. Compared with the great hostiles, *Asuras* for instance, the popular idea of the devil in Christianity is but a grotesque caricature. Hostile beings influence our lives constantly, unseen and unawares, and are the cause of all evil, corruption and perversion, for that is what they revel in. They resist every effort to change the world or oneself for the better as that goes against their interests. This means that they are the arch-enemies of any kind of spiritual discipline and of the transformation of the world.

Secondly, Sri Aurobindo and the Mother rarely talked about themselves in public. The intimate details known about them are mainly found in personal writings, letters and conversations published after their passing away. When they could not avoid mentioning themselves, they did so with great discretion, though the truth sometimes compelled them to say who they were and what they stood for.

What they stood for, we know now. We know Mirra realised that a new chapter in the evolution of the planet was going to be written – and so did Sri Aurobindo, of course. But what seems to be little remembered about the latter is that he represents a totally new chapter in Indian philosophy and spirituality. We have already seen how he distanced himself from the Buddha and from Shankara. "I seek a text and a *Shastra* [scripture]", he wrote, "that is not subject to interpolation, modification and replacement, that moth and white ant cannot destroy, that the earth cannot bury nor Time mutilate ... I believe that Veda to be the foundation of the *Sanatan Dharma* [the eternal law]; I

---

15. Sri Aurobindo: *On Himself,* p. 153.

believe it to be the concealed divinity within Hinduism, – but a veil has to be drawn aside, a curtain has to be lifted. I believe it to be knowable and discoverable. I believe the future of India and the world to depend on its discovery and on its application, not to the renunciation of life, but to life in the world and among men."[16] – "It is irrelevant to me what Max Müller thinks of the Veda or what Sayana thinks of the Veda. I should prefer to know what the Veda has to say for itself and, if there is any light there on the unknown or on the infinite, to follow the ray till I come face to face with that which it illumines."[17]

Reflecting upon himself in an early note, he wrote: "You will find disputants questioning your system on the ground that it is not consistent with this or that Shastra or this or that great authority, whether philosopher, saint or Avatar. Remember then that realisation and[18] experience are alone of essential importance. What Shankara argued or Vivekananda conceived intellectually about existence or even what Ramakrishna stated from his multitudinous and varied realisation, is only of value to you so far as you [are] moved by God to accept and renew it in your own experience. The opinions of thinkers and saints and Avatars should be accepted as hints, not as fetters. What matters to you is what you have seen or what God in his universal personality or impersonally or again personally in some teacher, guru or pathfinder undertakes to show you in the path of Yoga."[19]

Sri Aurobindo wrote in the same vein to a disciple: "I have never disputed the truth of the old Yogas ... I recognise their truth in their own field and for their own purpose – the truth of the experience so far as it goes – though I am in no way bound to accept the truth of the mental philosophies founded on the experience. I similarly find that my Yoga is true in its own field – a larger field, as I think – and for its own purpose ... Only you

---

16. Sri Aurobindo: *Essays Divine and Human*, p. 65.
17. Ibid., p. 35.
18. As this was a handwritten note, the liberty is taken here to replace the sign "&" with "and" in order to facilitate the reading.
19. Sri Aurobindo: *Essays Divine and Human,* p. 105.

3. Turning Towards the Earth

say that the thing is impossible; but that is what is said about everything before it is done."[20]

In agreement with their principle of "a complete and catholic affirmation", Sri Aurobindo and the Mother would always be respectful and appreciative of other views, ancient as well as contemporary, and point to their essence. For, after all, everything in the world, being Brahman, must be a bearer of some truth, of some essential significance. But this did not mean that they were relativists pure and simple; on the contrary, they had a task to do, and the mental formulation of this task was only part of it. It is important, especially for Westerners, to keep in mind that "mental formulation" (philosophy) is secondary to praxis, to the practical, living realisation of knowledge. For the West, as we shall see further on, has been one-sided and therefore fundamentally flawed in its attitude towards Existence. Its approach to things has been mental through and through, it has been an exercise of the mind; the living, the praxis, the spiritual realisation of the knowledge it gained was for many centuries limited to prescriptions by a Church and to not much more than religious ethics. "Truth of philosophy", noted Sri Aurobindo, "is of a merely theoretical value unless it can be lived."[21]

The freedom Sri Aurobindo and Mirra exacted for themselves has its manifesto on the very first page of the *Essays on the Gita*, in which Sri Aurobindo in his turn, after the great Indian philosophers of earlier times, interprets what is probably the most revered and undoubtedly the most commented upon text of the *Shastra*. He writes, not mincing his words: "The world abounds with Scriptures sacred and profane, with revelations and half-revelations, with religions and philosophies, sects and schools and systems. To these the many minds of a half-ripe knowledge or no knowledge at all attach themselves with exclusiveness and passion and will have it that this or the other book is alone the eternal Word of God and all others are either impostures or at best imperfectly inspired, that this or that

---

20. Sri Aurobindo: *On Himself*, p. 127.
21. Sri Aurobindo: *Essays in Philosophy and Yoga*, p. 108.

philosophy is the last word of the reasoning intellect and other systems are either errors or saved only by such partial truth in them as links them to the one true philosophical cult. Even the discoveries of physical Science have been elevated into a creed and in its name religion and spirituality banned as ignorance and superstition, philosophy as frippery and moonshine …

"Mankind seems now indeed inclined to grow a little modester and wiser; we no longer slay our fellows in the name of God's truth or because they have minds differently trained or differently constituted from ours; we are less ready to curse and revile our neighbour because he is wicked or presumptuous enough to differ from us in opinion; we are ready even to admit that Truth is everywhere and cannot be our sole monopoly; we are beginning to look at other religions and philosophies for the truth and help they contain and no longer merely in order to damn them as false or criticise what we conceive to be their errors. But we are still apt to declare that our truth gives us *the* supreme knowledge which other religions or philosophies have missed or only imperfectly grasped so that they deal with subsidiary and inferior aspects of the truth of things or can merely prepare less evolved minds for the heights to which we have arrived. And we are still prone to force upon ourselves or others the whole sacred mass of the book or gospel we admire, insisting that all shall be accepted as eternally valid truth and no iota or underline or diaeresis denied its part of the plenary inspiration."[22]

This paragraph alone should prevent Aurobindonians from being sectarians or fanatics. But once again, this is not an incentive to complete relativism. As (re)discovered by some mainstream schools of present-day philosophy, Mind has no grasp on essentials; therefore it can never know Truth and is always dependent on the prevalent ways of thinking peculiar to the culture and time it is active in. Yet to discover the truth behind a given view one has to follow a discipline, especially if the view is spiritual, which every world-view ultimately is. Following a spiritual discipline demands the commitment of

---

22. Sri Aurobindo: *Essays on the Gita,* pp 3, 4.

the whole person for a considerable period of time, if not for the remainder of his or her life. The conclusion is that to follow a teaching intended to change things – in Sri Aurobindo and the Mother's case to change the world – one has to be as broad-minded as the problem one intends to tackle (the world) is large, while inwardly remaining concentrated on the task of complete transformation (integral yoga) in a total dedication. We will briefly touch upon this later.

"Avatars Still Come"

The following quotations are from Sri Aurobindo's letters to disciples:

- "I had my past and the world's past to assimilate and overpass before I could find and found the future."[23]

- "As for the Mother and myself, we have had to try all ways, follow all methods, to surmount mountains of difficulties, a far heavier burden to bear than you or anybody else in the Ashram or outside, far more difficult conditions, battles to fight, wounds to endure, ways to cleave through impenetrable morass and desert and forest, hostile masses to conquer – a work such as, I am certain, none else had to do before us. For the Leader of the Way in a work like ours has not only to bring down and represent and embody the Divine, but to represent too the ascending element in humanity and to bear the burden of humanity to the full and experience, not in a mere play or Lila but in grim earnest, all the obstruction, difficulty, opposition, baffled and hampered and only slowly victorious labour which are possible on the path."[24]

- "No difficulty that can come on the Sadhak[25] but has faced

---
23. Sri Aurobindo: *On Himself*, p. 78.
24. Sri Aurobindo: *On Himself*, p. 464.
25. A "sadhak", feminine "sadhika", is a person who practices "sadhana", i.e. a spiritual discipline.

us on the path ... It is in fact to ensure an easier path to others hereafter that we have borne that burden."[26]

- "I have borne every attack which human beings have borne, otherwise I would be unable to assure anybody: 'This too can be conquered.' At least I would have no right to say so ... The Divine, when he takes on the burden of terrestrial nature, takes it fully, sincerely and without any conjuring tricks or pretence. If he has something behind him which emerges always out of the coverings, it is the same thing in essence even if greater in degree, that there is behind others – and it is to awaken that that he is there."[27]

- "It is only divine Love which can bear the burden I have to bear, that all have to bear who have sacrificed everything else to the one aim of uplifting earth out of its darkness towards the Divine."[28]

- "As for faith, you write as if I never had a doubt or any difficulty. I have had worse than any human mind can think of. It is not because I have ignored difficulties, but because I have seen them more clearly, experienced them on a larger scale than anyone living now or before me that, having faced and measured them, I am sure of the results of my work. But even if I still saw the chance that it might come to nothing (which is impossible), I would go on unperturbed, because I would still have done to the best of my power the work that I have to do, and what is so done always counts in the economy of the universe."[29]

These words, in all their dramatic directness, disclose the essence of avatarhood better than any comment or paraphrase could do. Here the Avatar is giving us in his own words an idea of what it means for him to take on a human body in order to bring the evolution a step further. Sri Aurobindo is speaking

---
26. Sri Aurobindo: *On Himself*, p. 465.
27. Nirodbaran: *Correspondence with Sri Aurobindo*, p. 176.
28. Ibid., p. 152.
29. Nirodbaran: *Correspondence with Sri Aurobindo*, p. 154.

3. Turning Towards the Earth

not only in his own name but also in the name of the Mother. Their path was identical, their task was the same, their sufferings were equally gruesome. The Mother rarely spoke about the torment until later, in the conversations that constitute the *Agenda*.

In the previous chapter we have defined an Avatar as the direct incarnation of the Divine in his manifestation to make the next higher step in evolution possible. "The Divine", wrote Sri Aurobindo, "puts on an appearance of humanity, assumes the outward human nature in order to tread the path and show it to human beings, but does not cease to be the Divine. It is a manifestation that takes place, a manifestation of a growing divine consciousness, not human turning into divine."[30]

The concept of the Avatar is actually very well known in the West, for it defines the being and mission of Christ.[31] The difference with the Hindu concept lies in the fact that Christianity acknowledges only one Avatar, while in the Hindu view there is a succession of Avatars which furthers the earthly evolution. So extraordinary, so "unhuman" is the divine embodiment to the human understanding that the interpretation of the person and role of Christ has been the cause of numerous Christian heresies. Some interpretations saw Christ as purely human, others as exclusively divine, with every possible combination of both views in between. This groping for the truth about the Avatar seems to be a common phenomenon, for one finds the same kind of "theological" interpretations in the Hindu assessments of Rama and Krishna – and in the assessments of Sri Aurobindo and the Mother by their disciples, as reflected in the aforementioned quotations. Some disciples obviously had doubts about the accomplishment of Sri Aurobindo's avataric mission, in some cases reducing him to a fallible human being; others supposed that he, being divine, could not really suffer or doubt, but was only putting on a show, a *lila*. And then there were the vacillations between those two extreme viewpoints,

---

30. Sri Aurobindo: *On the Mother*, p. 48.
31. In his writings, Sri Aurobindo usually named Christ as an Avatar together with Krishna and Buddha.

often in one and the same disciple. The spectrum of attitudes towards the Mother was exactly the same: some considered her wholly divine and expected her to fulfil all their demands in the blink of an eye, others would not accept or could not discern the divinity in her human personality.

We may summarise Sri Aurobindo's statements about himself as Avatar in the following way. The Avatar has to assimilate the world's past in order to make the new evolutionary quantum jump possible. He, "the Leader of the Way", has to take up the human condition as it is, carry out the Yoga of the world and bring it into unexplored evolutionary territory. This superhuman task is more difficult, more vast and more painful than any ordinary human being would be able to stand and accomplish. It has to be performed "in grim earnest", for the Avatar's difficulties and suffering are real. The difficulties must be conquered to make them conquerable by the ones who will follow on the newly paved path. "Only divine Love" can bear such a burden. His greater knowledge gives him also a deeper insight into the "impossibility" of the task, for if it were not impossible for ordinary human beings, he would not have to come to do it.

A child once asked the Mother: "Mother, are you God?" The Mother, ever smiling, answered: "Yes, my child, and so are you." The human being too has the divine in itself. The difference between the Avatar and the ordinary human being consists in the fact that the Avatar is a direct embodiment of the Divine – "he has something behind him which emerges always out of the [human] coverings" – while the Divine portion in the human being has chosen to participate in the adventure of the evolution and therefore has become "temporarily" ignorant of its essence. As the Avatar is born of human parents in a human *adhara*, he may not be immediately aware of his avatarhood. In his youth Sri Aurobindo was, according to his own statement, an agnostic; he probably united with his true Being during the first years of his stay in Pondicherry, between 1910 and 1914. The Mother was aware of her uniqueness even in early childhood. She was told by Madame Théon during her occultist days in Tlemcen that she was an incarnation of the Universal Mother, and this was confirmed by Sri Aurobindo after their first meeting. Several diary entries in October 1914 bear witness to her conscious unification with the Great Mother. Essentially, Sri Aurobindo and the Mother were the double-poled supramental Avatar, descended to create a divine world. "The Mother's consciousness and mine are the same", asserted Sri Aurobindo; "the one Divine Consciousness in two, because that is necessary for the play."[32]

Those who feel that the suffering Sri Aurobindo mentions is perhaps exaggerated might contemplate for a moment what it must have meant to be nailed to a cross knowing beforehand that such an experience is awaiting you. Yet, the crucifixion of Christ was only the climax of his Avatarhood,[33] for the whole life of an Avatar is dedicated to the effort of transforming humanity.

Sri Aurobindo gave one of the most striking accounts of his avataric toil in an autobiographic poem written in 1935 and called "A God's Labour".

> He who would bring the heavens here
>   Must descend himself into clay
> And the burden of earthly nature bear
>   And tread the dolorous way ...
>
> My gaping wounds are a thousand and one
>   And the Titan kings assail,
> But I cannot rest till my task is done
>   And wrought the eternal will ...
>
> I have delved through the dumb Earth's dreadful heart
>   And heard her black mass' bell.
> I have seen the source whence her agonies part
>   And the inner reason of hell ...[34]

---

32. Sri Aurobindo: *On Himself,* p. 456.
33. The Mother referred to it explicitly during one of the most distressing moments of her Yoga.
34. Sri Aurobindo: *Collected Poems,* pp. 99 ff.

If ever there was an "avataric" poem, it is this one, regrettably too long to be quoted in full. Not that one saw much of the suffering. Sri Aurobindo had trained his body to such a degree that all the few people who had access to him saw was him sitting there in that big armchair, staring at the wall in front of him. But when in the years after 1958 the Mother worked on the transformation of her body, which had become the body of the world, then at times her suffering became quite evident.

Still, nothing could prevent the Avatar from doing the job he/she had come to do and the spirit remained unflaggingly radical. "Let all men jeer at me if they will or all Hell fall upon me if it will for my presumption [to change the world], – I go on till I conquer or perish. This is the spirit in which I seek the Supermind, no hunting for greatness for myself or others."[35] Sri Aurobindo is mostly seen as a sage, a calm, self-mastered, sattwic *mahayogi* (great yogi), a visionary, a philosopher, a poet, but he is seldom seen as the Warrior he was. It is, however, his warriorhood that made the rest possible. The last Avatar of the Hindus, Kalki, is represented as riding a white, winged horse and brandishing the flaming sword of Truth. But "too much importance need not be attached to the details about Kalki", wrote Sri Aurobindo in a letter, "they are rather symbolic than an attempt to prophesy details of future history. What is expressed is something that has to come, but it is symbolically indicated, no more."[36] Kalki, of course, was Sri Aurobindo – but people in the present time do not realise that Kalki had already come to wage his battle. For he had not come as expected in one male body, but in the bodies of Sri Aurobindo and the Mother, who was herself no less a warrior. For are two of the personalities of the Great Mother not Durga and Kali?

> Out, out with the mind and its candle flares,
>   Light, light the suns that never die.
> For me the cry of the seraph stars
>   And the forms of the gods for my naked eye![37]

---
35. Sri Aurobindo: *On Himself,* p. 144.
36. Sri Aurobindo: *Letters on Yoga,* p. 403.
37. Sri Aurobindo: *Collected Poems,* p. 589.

3. Turning Towards the Earth

This too was the voice of the soft-spoken Sri Aurobindo – who had risen far beyond human dimensions, as he relates in the autobiographical parts of his epic poem *Savitri*. Nevertheless, this should not lead us to the conclusion that the path he was hewing through the virgin forest of the future – a simile often used by him and by the Mother – was all daring and improvisation. On the contrary, he "cast his deeds like bronze to front the years",[38] patient, undaunted, with the sturdy perseverance of the great builders.

"I think I can say that I have been testing day and night for years upon years more scrupulously than any scientist his theory or his method on the physical plane", he wrote. "That is why I am not alarmed by the aspect of the world around me or disconcerted by the often successful fury of the adverse Forces [note the capital letter] who increase in their rage as the Light comes nearer and nearer to the field of earth and Matter."[39] This letter was written somewhere around 1935, but such had been his attitude from the beginning. "Adhering still to the essential rigorous method of science, though not to its purely physical instrumentation, scrutinising, experimenting, holding nothing for established which cannot be scrupulously and universally verified, we shall still arrive at supraphysical certitudes. There are other means, there are greater approaches, but this line of access too can lead to the one universal truth."[40]

"To form no conclusions which are not justified by observation and reasoning, to doubt everything until it is proved but to deny nothing until it is disproved, to be always ready to reconsider old conclusions in the light of new facts, to give a candid consideration to every new idea or old idea revived if it deserves a hearing, no matter how contradictory it may be of previously ascertained experience or previously formed conclusion, is the sceptical temper, the temper of the inquirer, the true scientist, the untrammelled thinker."[41] This was Sri Aurobindo.

---

38. Sri Aurobindo: *Savitri*, p. 45.
39. Sri Aurobindo: *On Himself*, p. 469.
40. Sri Aurobindo: *Essays in Philosophy and Yoga*, p. 195.
41. Sri Aurobindo: *Essays Divine and Human*, p. 23.

Few have evaluated science and materialism with as much clarity and intuitive insight as Sri Aurobindo and the Mother. They perceived the force lines of history and had a clear appreciation of their substance and role. To give but one example, Sri Aurobindo wrote in the opening pages of *The Life Divine:* "The touch of Earth is always reinvigorating to the son of Earth, even when he seeks a supraphysical Knowledge. It may even be said the supraphysical can only be really mastered in its fullness – to its heights we can always reach – when we keep our feet firmly on the physical. 'Earth is his footing', says the Upanishad whenever it images the Self that manifests in the universe. And it is certainly the fact that the wider we extend and the surer we make our knowledge of the physical world, the wider and surer becomes our foundation for the higher knowledge, even the highest, even the Brahmavidya [knowledge of Brahman]."[42]

Evidently, Sri Aurobindo and the Mother could not agree with the turn taken by science into scientism[43] which flattened, "collapsed" the dimensions of being into a single one. A substantial volume could be written about their insights into this subject. Here the following prediction will have to suffice: "If modern Materialism were simply an unintelligent acquiescence in the material life, the advance might be indefinitely delayed. But since its very soul is the search for Knowledge, it will be unable to cry a halt; as it reaches the barriers of sense-knowledge and of the reasoning from sense-knowledge, its very rush will carry it beyond and the rapidity and sureness with which it has embraced the visible universe is only an earnest of the energy and success which we may hope to see repeated in the conquest of what lies beyond, once the stride is taken that crosses the barrier. We see already that advance in its obscure beginnings."[44] Science is moving more and more into the realm of the invisible which by definition is the occult – a mathematical formula does

---

42. Sri Aurobindo: *The Life Divine,* p. 11.
43. In *Beyond the Post-Modern Mind* (p. 146) Huston Smith defines "scientism" as "the drawing of conclusions from science that do not logically follow". He might have added: "and proclaiming those conclusions to be indubitable dogma".
44. Sri Aurobindo: *The Life Divine,* p. 13.

not make a neutron or a quark visible. And does the crisis of science – perhaps leading to a new and surprising scientific "paradigm" as predicted by Sri Aurobindo – not become apparent in works like John Horgan's widely commented upon *The End of Science* (1996)?

From 1950 till 1958, the Mother gave twice a week French evening classes to the youth of the Sri Aurobindo Ashram School, which had been founded by her during the Second World War. There the children could ask her any question that popped up in their head, and the Mother answered, drawing on her erudition, experience and vast occult and spiritual knowledge. She talked several times about high civilisations that had disappeared long ago. The progress of humanity moved in a kind of a spiral, she said, at times progressing, at times apparently regressing. Brilliant civilisations, "Golden Ages", some of which still live in humanity's memory, suddenly disappeared and were followed by long eras of darkness and primitivism. (We find this repeatedly confirmed in Sri Aurobindo.[45]) The high tides of civilisation were always accompanied by the variously formulated promise to mankind of a New Earth, of a Divine World, of a New Creation. But up to now, alas, "one has always fallen back."[46]

"Teachers of the law and love and oneness there must be, for by that way must come the ultimate salvation. But not till the time-spirit in man is ready can the inner and ultimate prevail over the outer and immediate reality. Christ and Buddha have come and gone, but it is Rudra[47] who still holds the world in the hollow of his hand. And meanwhile the fierce forward labour of mankind tormented and oppressed by the Powers that are profiteers of egoistic force and their servants cries for the sword of the Hero of the struggle and the word of its prophet."[48]

---

45. For instance on p. 869 of *The Life Divine:* "... this primitive stage, – if it is indeed such and not, in what we still see of it, a fall or a vestige, a relapse from a higher knowledge belonging to a previous cycle of civilisation or the debased remnants of a dead or obsolete culture ..."
46. The Mother: *Questions and Answers 1953,* 2 September.
47. Rudra is the terrible aspect of Shiva.
48. Sri Aurobindo: *Essays on the Gita,* p. 386.

– "Every time a god has taken a body, it has always been with the intention of transforming the earth and creating a new world. But till today, he has always had to give up his body without completing his work. And it has always been said that the earth was not ready and that men had not fulfilled the conditions necessary for the work to be achieved."[49]

It was Sri Aurobindo and the Mother's warrior will that there would be no falling back this time. "I have no intention", wrote Sri Aurobindo, "of giving my sanction to a new edition of the old fiasco, a partial and transient spiritual opening within with no true and radical change in the external nature."[50] He also wrote: "A partial realisation, something mixed and inconclusive, does not meet the demand I make on life and Yoga."[51] And: "Neither antiquity nor modernity can be the test of truth or the test of usefulness. All the Rishis do not belong to the past; the Avatars still come; revelation still continues."[52]

The Integral Yoga

The path through the virgin forest had to be cleared, the method had to be found, the "yoga" had to be built up. We know that Mirra as well as Sri Aurobindo were powerfully aided by extramaterial beings who watched over their perilous road, which they followed with total dedication. But it was ultimately the embodied double Avatar who had to do the job for which he/she had come, consisting in developing a new spiritual *modus operandi* in order to work out a new spiritual realisation: the supramental transformation of the body, of the material substance of the earth.

One may get an idea of their struggle's countless unforeseen challenges and of the heroism required of "the finders of the Way"[53] in Nirodbaran's *Correspondence with Sri Aurobindo* for

---

49. *Words of the Mother,* CWM 15, p. 299.
50. Sri Aurobindo: *Letters on Yoga,* p. 1306.
51. Sri Aurobindo: *On Himself* p. 107.
52. Sri Aurobindo: *Essays Divine and Human,* p. 50.
53. Sri Aurobindo: *On Himself,* p. 465.

3. Turning Towards the Earth

the period 1933-38, in Sri Aurobindo's autobiographical poems and parts of *Savitri* (especially the first three Books), and in *Mother's Agenda*, conversations with the Mother in the last twelve years of her life.[54] Their establishing of the path of the "Integral Yoga", as Sri Aurobindo named it – in the beginning he also sometimes called it *Purna Yoga* (complete yoga) or "Synthetic Yoga" – would allow others to follow in their footsteps; for creating a divine life necessitated collaboration from the flower of humanity. Sri Aurobindo would call the Integral Yoga "the path I had opened, as Christ, Krishna, Buddha, Chaitanya, etc. opened theirs."[55]

A systematic yoga is only possible when the path as well as the goal are known and determined. The goal of the Integral Yoga is known but not determined. The goal is the realisation of a supramental body on the Earth; what a supramental body will be like is (more or less) known; but its realisation is not fixed, not determined, as up to now nobody has concretely existed in a supramental body. And didn't Sri Aurobindo time and again refuse to define Supermind so as not to limit it by mental formations? Besides, the Integral Yoga is as complex as its object, which is the whole world, and as every practitioner of the Yoga is different, his or her approach has to be different. We may therefore conclude that the path of the Integral Yoga has been cleared up to a certain point, i.e. as far as Sri Aurobindo and the Mother went on it, that its method has been established in principle, but that it will be fully determined only when the first supramental beings appear on this planet and the whole path will be perceptible and describable.

Sri Aurobindo's words in *The Life Divine* leave no doubt in this matter: "... Evolutionary [and evolving] Nature is not a logical series of separate segments; it is a totality of ascending powers of being which interpenetrate and dovetail and exercise in their action on each other a power of mutual modification ...

---

54. See also the books by Georges Van Vrekhem mentioned in a footnote in the first chapter, where the trajectory of Sri Aurobindo and Mother's yoga is for the first time described in its completeness.
55. Nirodbaran: *Correspondence with Sri Aurobindo*, p. 172.

This interaction creates an abundant number of different intermediate and interlocked degrees of the force and consciousness of being, but it also makes it difficult to bring about a complete integration of all the powers under the full control of any one power. For this reason there is not actually a series of simple clear-cut and successive stages in the individual's evolution; there is instead a complexity and a partly determinate, partly confused comprehensiveness of the [yogic] movement."[56] And he goes on to compare the yogic development to "a tide or a mounting flux, the leading fringe of which touches the higher degrees of a cliff or hill while the rest is still below", and to "an army advancing in columns which annexes new ground, while the main body is still behind in a territory overrun but too large to be effectively occupied, so that there has to be a frequent halt and partial return to the traversed areas for consolidation and assurance of the hold on the occupied country and assimilation of its people."[57]

"All Yoga is in its very nature a means of passing out of our surface consciousness of limitation and ignorance into a larger and deeper Reality of ourselves and the world and some supreme or total Existence now veiled to us by this surface. There is a Reality which underlies everything, permeates perhaps everything, is perhaps everything but in quite another way than the world now seen by us; to it we are obscurely moving by our thought, life and actions; we attempt to understand and approach it by our religion and philosophy, at last we touch it directly in some partial or, it may be, some complete spiritual experience. It is that spiritual experience, it is the method, it is the attainment of this realisation that we call Yoga."[58] This being the general principle, what specifically is Integral Yoga?

"What is Integral Yoga? It is the way of complete God-realisation, a complete Self-realisation, a complete fulfilment of our being and consciousness, a complete transformation of our nature – and this implies a complete perfection of life here and

---

56. Sri Aurobindo: *The Life Divine*, pp. 955-56.
57. Ibid.
58. Sri Aurobindo: *Essays Divine and Human*, p. 361.

not only a return to an eternal perfection elsewhere. This is the object, but in the method also there is the same integrality, for the entirety of the object cannot be accomplished without an entirety in the method, a complete turning, opening, self-giving of our being and nature in all its parts, ways, movements to that which we realise. Our mind, will, heart, life, body, our outer and inner and inmost existence, our superconscious and subconscious as well as our conscious parts, must all be thus given, must all become a means, a field of this realisation and transformation and participate in the illumination and the change from a human into a divine consciousness and nature."[59]

For the general reader a text like this may not be easy to fathom at one go. Each sentence, each phrase has its subtle resonances, and Sri Aurobindo's sonorous language evokes a globality that has to be intuited to be properly apprehended. On the other hand, quoting Sri Aurobindo's own words is the safest way not to distort or dilute his meaning. The historian Arthur Lovejoy wrote in his book on the Great Chain of Being: "... [The citation of illustrative passages from the original authors] will, I dare say, seem to some readers too abundant. But in my own reading of works of this character [i.e. historic] I have often been exasperated by finding *précis* or paraphrases where I desiderated the actual language of the authors whose ideas were under consideration; and my rule has therefore been to give the words of relevant texts as fully as was consistent with reasonable brevity."[60]

So, how better to outline the newness of the Integral Yoga than in Sri Aurobindo's own words? "[The Integral Yoga] is new as compared with the old Yogas:

"1. Because it aims not at a departure out of world and life into Heaven and Nirvana, but at a change of life and existence, not as something subordinate or incidental, but as a distinct and central object. If there is a descent in other Yogas, yet it is only an incident on the way or resulting from the ascent – the ascent is the real thing. Here the ascent is the first step, but it is

---
59. Ibid., p. 358.
60. From the preface of Arthur Lovejoy's: *The Great Chain of Being*.

[handwritten note at top: We do not ascend! Our new consciousness descends to meet us.]

a means for the descent. It is the descent of the new consciousness [Supermind] attained by the ascent that is the stamp and seal of the Sadhana. Even the Tantra and Vaishnavism end in the release from life; here the object is the divine fulfilment of life.

"2. Because the object sought after is not an individual achievement of divine realisation for the sake of the individual, but something to be gained for the earth-consciousness here, a cosmic, not solely a supra-cosmic achievement. The thing to be gained also is the bringing in of a Power of Consciousness (the Supramental) not yet organised or active directly in earth-nature, even in the spiritual life, but yet to be organised and made directly active.

"3. Because a method has been recognised for achieving this purpose which is as total and integral as the aim set before it, viz., the total and integral change of the consciousness and nature, taking up old methods but only as a part action and present aid to others that are distinctive. I have not found this method (as a whole) or anything like it professed or realised in the old Yogas. If I had, I should not have wasted my time in hewing out a road and in thirty years of search and inner creation when I could have hastened home safely to my goal in an easy canter over paths already blazed out, laid down, perfectly mapped, macadamised, made secure and public. Our Yoga is not a retreading of old walks, but a spiritual adventure."[61]

The radical newness of this stance has been noted by many commentators. In connection with the second point above, for instance, we quote Chitta Ranjan Goswami in *Sri Aurobindo's Concept of the Superman:* "... In a very important respect Sri Aurobindo's conception of the superman differs from anything conceived in the past. Sri Aurobindo thinks not only of individual superman but also of a race of supermen. The collectivity is conceived to evolve gradually to a higher stage of life and being. When the *Bodhisattva* resolves not to get into *Nirvana* (final fulfilment) until all others are made ready for the same, the stress is purely on individual liberation, one by one. The idea

---

61. Sri Aurobindo: *On Himself,* p. 109.

of a society of the liberated is altogether absent in the Indian tradition."[62]

The goal of the Integral Yoga, according to Sri Aurobindo, was "to become one in our absolute being with the ineffable Divine and in the manifestation a free movement of his being, power, consciousness and self-realising joy, to grow into a divine Truth-consciousness beyond mind, into a Light beyond all human or earthly lights, into a Power to which the greatest strengths of men are a weakness, into the wisdom of an infallible gnosis and the mastery of an unerring and unfailing divinity of Will, into a Bliss beside which all human pleasure is as the broken reflection of a candle-flame to the all-pervading splendour of an imperishable sun, but all this not for our own sake [but] for the pleasure of the Divine Beloved, this is the goal and the crown of the supramental path of Yoga."[63]

"Our Yoga is a Yoga of transformation", he wrote, "but a transformation of the whole consciousness and the whole nature from the top to the bottom."[64] This is explicit. A spiritual effort of this kind cannot bear fruit unless every part of the human being is fully open to the divine influence and direction. It is the Great Mother, the Divine Creatrix, who is the origin *fons et origo,* of the whole manifestation – who *is* the whole manifestation, including this very special Earth. The evolution of the Earth is the Yoga of the Earth; the supramental or Integral Yoga is actually a revolutionary acceleration of the evolution. This throws some light on the reason why the Supramental Avatar was not only male but also female in embodiment though one in Consciousness: the Great Mother had to be directly present, in person, at the perilous juncture of the transition and transformation of the lower into the higher hemisphere. Sri Aurobindo and the Mother had tried out many ways to construct the new path; in the end Sri Aurobindo confided the Integral Yoga entirely to the Mother, who was doing it herself, literally, in every person turned towards her. For every soul on

---
62. Chitta Ranjan Goswami: *Sri Aurobindo's Concept of the Superman,* p. 35.
63. Sri Aurobindo: *Essays Divine and Human,* p. 364.
64. Ibid., p. 371.

earth "is a portion of the Divine Mother"[65]; and: "It is only those who are capable by aspiration and meditation on the Mother to open and receive her action and working within that can succeed in this Yoga."[66]

A "Yoga with these dimensions and this degree of difficulty is not meant for everybody, one has to be called to it. "First be sure of the call and of thy soul's answer ... Imagine not the way is easy; the way is long, arduous, dangerous, difficult. At every step is an ambush, at every turn a pitfall. A thousand seen and unseen enemies will start up against thee, terrible in subtlety against thy ignorance, formidable in power against thy weakness. And when with pain thou hast destroyed them, thousands will surge up to take their place. Hell will vomit its hordes to oppose thee and enring and wound and menace; Heaven will meet thee with its pitiless tests and its cold luminous denials. Thou shalt find thyself alone in thy anguish, the demons furious in thy path, the Gods unwilling above thee. Ancient and powerful, cruel, unvanquished and close and innumerable are the dark and dreadful Powers that profit by the reign of Night and Ignorance and would have no change and are hostile. Aloof, slow to arrive, far-off and few and brief in their visits are the Bright Ones who are willing or permitted to succour. Each step forward is a battle ..."[67] All this was reported from Sri Aurobindo's personal experience and reminds us in prose of what he sang elsewhere in that sweet and terrible poem, *A God's Labour.*

The expected result should be, we may suppose, at least equivalent to the magnitude of the effort. "The boon that we have asked from the Supreme is the greatest that the earth can ask from the Highest, the change that is most difficult to realise, the most exacting in its conditions. It is nothing less than the descent of the supreme Truth and Power into Matter, the supramental established in the material plane and consciousness in the material world and an integral transformation down

---

65. Sri Aurobindo: *On the Mother,* p. 79.
66. Ibid., p. 121.
67. Sri Aurobindo: *Essays Divine and Human,* pp. 155-56.

to the very principle of Matter. Only a supreme Grace can effect this miracle"[68] – as only a supreme Grace can bring this Yoga of physical transformation to fruition.

"This Thing of Capital Importance ..."

"If Supermind descends upon the earth, it will bring necessarily the divine life with it and establish it here ... The manifestation of a supramental truth-consciousness is therefore the capital reality that will make the divine life possible,"[69] wrote Sri Aurobindo. "If Supermind descends ...", "if the supramental comes down ..." It was *the* condition, the *conditio sine qua non*, the aim of Sri Aurobindo and the Mother's whole effort from the beginning of their destined collaboration. The human being had appeared in evolution because of the descent of Mind, the rational level of the mental consciousness, into the earth-atmosphere. Now the condition for the appearance of the supramental being, the species beyond the human being, was the descent of Supermind. "The ancient dawns of human knowledge have left us their witness to this constant aspiration ..."[70]

"I am not trying to change the world all at once but only to bring down centrally something into it, it has not yet, a new consciousness and power,"[71] wrote Sri Aurobindo in a letter. And in another one, of October 1935: "The present business is to bring down and establish the Supermind, not to explain it."[72] – "I know that the supramental Descent is inevitable – I have faith in view of my experience that the time can and should be now and not in a later age ... But even if I knew it to be for a later time, I would not swerve from my path or be discouraged or flag in my labour. Formerly I might have been, but not *now* – after all the path I have traversed. When one is sure of the Truth, or even when one believes the thing one pursues

---
68. Ibid., p. 359.
69. Sri Aurobindo: *Essays in Philosophy and Yoga*, p. 560.
70. Sri Aurobindo: *The Life Divine*, p. 1.
71. Sri Aurobindo: *On Himself*, p. 166.
72. Ibid., p. 164.

to be the only possible solution, one does not stipulate for an immediate success, one travels towards the Light taking as well worthwhile and facing every risk of the adventure. Still, like you, it is now, in this life that I insist on it and not in another or in the hereafter."[73] (30.8.1932)

"I know with absolute certitude that the supramental is a truth and that its advent is in the very nature of things inevitable. The question is as to the when and the how. That also is decided and predestined from somewhere above; but it is here being fought out amid a rather grim clash of conflicting forces. For in the terrestrial world the predetermined result is hidden and what we see is a whirl of possibilities and forces attempting to achieve something with the destiny of it all concealed from human eyes. This is, however, certain that a number of souls have been sent to see that it shall be now. That is the situation. My faith and will are for the now."[74] (25.12.1934)

"The hour of the realisations is near", noted Mirra in her diary as early as September 1914.

"A new light shall break upon the earth.

"A new world shall be born.

"And the things that were promised shall be fulfilled."[75] However, the previous pages should have made clear that the realisation of Sri Aurobindo and the Mother's endeavour would be difficult and complex – and unforeseeable. Yes, the Supramental Consciousness would descend, but later than expected and after some daunting obstacles and dramatic developments.

---

73. Ibid., p. 469.
74. Ibid., p. 167.
75. The Mother: *Prayers and Meditations*, p. 273

4.
A First Sketch of Supermanhood

> ... *From the new race would be recruited the race of supramental beings who would appear as the leaders of the evolution in earth-nature.*[1]
>
> – Sri Aurobindo

Sri Aurobindo and the Mother's whole effort was focused on the descent of the Supermind into the earth-consciousness, the crucial and basic event that would found the future and that they wanted to effect as soon as possible. To that end Sri Aurobindo withdrew into his apartment after the "Siddhi Day" of 1926, never to leave it again. To that end the Mother, now in charge of the Sri Aurobindo Ashram, worked tirelessly among the steadily growing number of disciples, in order to prepare humanity and the Earth they represented. In 1935 Sri Aurobindo announced, in his delightful correspondence with Nirodbaran, that he had good hope to bring "the supramental Whale" down soon.[2]

But the Hostiles were vigilant. When in 1938 Sri Aurobindo and the Mother seemed convinced that the Great Event would take place before the end of the year, Sri Aurobindo was the object of a direct attack and broke his thigh; the work towards the chief aim had to be interrupted. Then the Second World War erupted and needed all Sri Aurobindo and the Mother's attention and even their occult interventions to ensure that the descent would remain possible, that the anti-evolutionary forces would not carry the day and postpone the advent of the New World for centuries if not for millennia.

---

1. Sri Aurobindo: *Essays in Philosophy and Yoga*, p. 585.
2. Nirodbaran: *Correspondence with Sri Aurobindo*, p. 321.

According to Sri Aurobindo the global situation remained critical after the war, even more dangerous than during the worldwide conflagration. Commenting on the war in Korea, Sri Aurobindo judged "the situation as grave as it can be". He seems, moreover, to have been confronted with a central obstacle in the Inconscient. He wrote in 1947 that the Yoga had "come down against the bedrock of Inconscience."[3] From the same year are the following words: "At the present stage the progressive supramentalisation of the Overmind is the first immediate preoccupation and a second is the lightening of *the heavy resistance of the Inconscient* and the support it gives to human ignorance which is always the main obstacle in any attempt to change the world or even to change oneself."[4] One may remember the extracts in the preceding chapter of the account of his efforts contained in "A God's Labour". To those we add a few lines from *Savitri:*

> Into the abysmal secrecy he came
> Where darkness peers from her mattress, grey and nude,
> And stood on the last locked subconscients floor
> Where Being slept unconscious of its thoughts
> And built the world not knowing what it built.
> There waiting its hour the future lay unknown,
> There is the record of the vanished stars.
> There in the slumber of the cosmic Will
> He saw the secret key of Nature's change.[5]

Nobody knows what that secret key was, but taking possession of it was certainly a deed only the Avatar himself could accomplish by means of a unique yogic master-act: a conscious descent into that "abysmal secrecy" – into death itself. The Mother knew about the problem, of course, and proposed to deal with it herself. But Sri Aurobindo forbade her, saying that her body was better suited than his to bear the ordeal of transformation, of supramentalisation. Their Yoga being an adventure

---
3. Sri Aurobindo: *On Himself* p. 169.
4. Ibid., p. 170 (emphasis added).
5. Sri Aurobindo: *Savitri*, p. 231.

into the unknown, they could not foresee everything; but they had reached a point where the main lines of development had become perceptible to them.

Such was the situation in the last months of Sri Aurobindo's life, when the Mother asked him to write a message for the *Bulletin of Physical Education*. She had founded a school during the war years, for many relatives of Ashramites, especially Bengalis, had descended on the Ashram in Pondicherry to seek shelter from the threatening Japanese. The children of those families had to be kept occupied – the serious inmates of the Ashram, concentrated on their *tapasya*, were far from happy with the children's presence! But the Sri Aurobindo Ashram was after all to be "a world in miniature", the fitting field for the work of transformation that was the aim of the Integral Yoga.

Sri Aurobindo, intensely occupied with completing *Savitri* (and with carrying out his avataric task on levels and in places of which we do not even have an inkling) did not write essayistic prose anymore, perhaps because for this kind of literary work his consciousness had to descend again to the ordinary human level. Besides, his eyesight had deteriorated and he had to dictate everything, poetry as well as prose, to Nirodbaran Talukdar, his amanuensis. But he could not refuse a request from the Mother. He dictated eight articles for the *Bulletin* between 30 December 1948 and the time he left his body, on 5 December 1950. The first article is the actual required message. Did he then write the other seven articles because he saw an opportunity or the necessity to make known a new development in the Integral Yoga? An editor of his *Collected Works* writes that "the series [of articles] was left unfinished". It certainly gives that impression. Yet, the contents of the articles are of immense importance, especially at the present time. This is what we will try to demonstrate.

"A New Humanity"

"I take the opportunity of the publication of this issue of the 'Bulletin d'Education Physique' of the Ashram", Sri Aurobindo began his message, "to give my blessings to the Journal and the Association – J.S.A.S.A. (Jeunesse Sportive de l'Ashram de Sri Aurobindo). In doing so I would like to dwell for a while on the deeper *raison d'être* of such Associations and especially the need and utility for the nation [i.e. the then newly independent India] of a widespread organisation of them and such sports or physical exercises as are practised here."[6] The Ashram not only represented, in miniature, the world, it also irradiated its attainments back into the world. This is an important fact without which the Mother's work cannot be fully appreciated.

Sri Aurobindo continues: "In our own time these sports, games and athletics have assumed a place and command a general interest such as was seen only in earlier times in countries like Greece,[7] where all sides of human activity were equally developed and the gymnasium, chariot-racing and other sports and athletics had the same importance on the physical side as on the mental side the Arts and poetry and the drama, and were especially stimulated and attended to by the civic authorities of the city state. It was Greece that made an institution of the Olympiad, and the recent re-establishment of the Olympiad as an international institution is a significant sign of the revival of the ancient spirit."[8]

In his *Twelve Years with Sri Aurobindo,* Nirodbaran reminisces: "When the *Bulletin of Sri Aurobindo International Centre of Education* was launched, the Mother wanted to initiate it with an article from Sri Aurobindo. Some days passed. She asked him if he had started writing it. He answered with a smile, 'No.' After a few days, she reminded him of the urgency. Then he began dictating on the value of sports and physical gymnastics

---

6. Sri Aurobindo: *Essays in Philosophy and Yoga*, p. 517.
7. As these articles were dictated, the capitalisation of some words and sometimes the punctuation are not always in accordance with Sri Aurobindo's usual way of writing.
8. Sri Aurobindo: *Essays in Philosophy and Yoga*, p. 517.

4. A First Sketch of Supermanhood

... As he was dictating, I marvelled at so much knowledge of Ancient Greece and Ancient India stored up somewhere in his superconscious memory and now pouring down at his command in a smooth flow. No notes were consulted, no books were needed, yet after a lapse of so many decades everything was fresh, spontaneous and recalled in vivid detail!"[9]

The second article is entitled *Perfection of the Body*. "A total perfection is the ultimate aim which we set before us, for our ideal is the Divine Life which we wish to create here, the life of the Spirit fulfilled on earth, life accomplishing its own spiritual transformation even here on earth in the conditions of the material universe. That cannot be unless the body too undergoes a transformation, unless its action and functioning attain to a supreme capacity and the perfection which is possible to it or which can be made possible ... The transformation is not a change into something purely subtle and spiritual to which Matter is in its nature repugnant and by which it is felt as an obstacle or as a shackle binding the Spirit; it takes up Matter as a form of the Spirit though now a form which conceals and turns it into a revealing instrument, it does not cast away the energies of Matter, its capacities, its methods; it brings out their hidden possibilities, uplifts, sublimates, discloses their intimate divinity. The divine life will reject nothing that is capable of divinisation; all is to be seized, exalted, made utterly perfect."[10]

In this second article, Sri Aurobindo again writes about the physical perfection that was the classical ideal, but then he suddenly takes a turn towards a perfection far beyond the physical: the supramental transformation of the body. "In the past the body has been regarded by spiritual seekers rather as an obstacle, as something to be overcome and discarded than as an instrument of spiritual perfection and a field of spiritual change ... Even in its fullest strength and force and greatest glory of beauty, it is still a flower of the material inconscience; the Inconscient is the soil from which it has grown and at every point opposes a narrow boundary to the extension of

---
9. Nirodbaran: *Twelve Years with Sri Aurobindo*, pp. 247-48
10. Sri Aurobindo: *Essays in Philosophy and Yoga*, pp. 521-22.

its powers and to any effort of radical self-exceeding. But if a divine life is possible on earth, then this self-exceeding must also be possible."[11]

The body is after all "the material basis ... the instrument we have to use", it is "the means of fulfilment of dharma",[12] even when dharma is changing into higher gear, into a totally new mode, when evolution itself begins to evolve. "If we could draw this power [of the Supermind] into the material world, our age-long dreams of human perfectibility, individual perfection, the perfectibility of the race, of society, inner mastery over self and a complete mastery, governance and utilisation of the forces of Nature could see at long last a prospect of total achievement."[13] In other words, the age-long dream of a truly Golden Age the Mother spoke of would become reality. (Gold is the colour of the Supermind.)

In the third article, Sri Aurobindo briefly summarises what we have tried to explain in Chapter 2: "It is indeed as a result of our evolution that we arrive at the possibility of this transformation. As Nature has evolved beyond Matter and manifested Life, beyond Life and manifested Mind, so she must evolve beyond Mind and manifest a consciousness and power of our existence free from the imperfection and limitation of our mental existence, a supramental or truth-consciousness, and able to develop the power and perfection of the spirit."[14]

And then comes the new development, not only in this series of articles but in the totality of the huge body of literature Sri Aurobindo had produced so far[15]: "It might be that the psychological change, a mastery of the nature by the soul, a transformation of the mind into a principle of light, of the life-force into power and purity would be the first approach, the first attempt to solve the problem, to escape beyond the merely

---

11. Ibid., p. 523.
12. Ibid., p. 521.
13. Ibid., p. 534.
14. Ibid., p. 536.
15. K.D. Sethna rightly called this series of articles, afterwards published as *The Supramental Manifestation upon Earth*, "in many senses a sequel to *The Life Divine*". See his *The Vision and Work of Sri Aurobindo*, p. 106.

4. A First Sketch of Supermanhood

human formula and establish something that could be called a divine life upon earth, *a first sketch of supermanhood, of a supramental living in the circumstances of the earth-nature.*" This is not what Sri Aurobindo and the Mother until then had consistently called "superman": "... It would not be the total transformation, the fullness of a divine life in a divine body. *There would be a body still human and indeed animal in its origin and fundamental character* and this would impose its own inevitable limitations on the higher parts of the embodied being."[16]

Sri Aurobindo then expands on this possibility: "It might be also that the transformation *might take place by stages,* there are powers of the nature still belonging to the mental region which are yet potentialities of a growing gnosis lifted beyond our human mentality and partaking of the light and power of the Divine and an ascent through these planes, a descent of them into the mental being might seem to be *the natural evolutionary course*". (What those "powers of the nature still belonging to the mental region" are we will see in the next section.) Sri Aurobindo stresses once again that by this he does not mean "superman". "Still these levels might become *stages of the ascent ...*"[17]

The gap, the quantum jump between the human and the supramental being is enormous. In the following pages will be quoted several passages from *The Life Divine* pointing in the direction of the necessity of a transitional being or several kinds of transitional beings. The fact that Sri Aurobindo here presents a new development in the Yoga of Transformation, when probably he had already taken the decision to descend voluntarily into death, is most remarkable and significant. As it will turn out, what he puts forward as a possibility was already partially realised in his own body.

In the fifth article of the series, he returns to this theme. "But Supermind alone has the truth-consciousness in full and, if this comes down and intervenes, mind, life and body too can attain to the full power of the truth in them and their full possibility

---

16. Sri Aurobindo: *Essays in Philosophy and Yoga*, p. 537 (emphasis added).
17. Ibid., pp. 537-38 (emphasis added).

of perfection. This, no doubt, would not take place at once, but *an evolutionary progress towards it could begin* and grow with increasing rapidity towards its fullness. All men might not reach that fullness till a later time, but still the human mind could come to stand perfected in the Light and *a new humanity* take its place as part of the new order.

"This is the possibility we have to examine. If it is destined to fulfil itself, if man is not doomed to remain always as a vassal of the Ignorance, the disabilities of the human mind on which we have dwelt are not such as must remain irredeemably in possession and binding for ever. It could develop higher means and instrumentalities, pass over the last borders of the Ignorance into a higher knowledge, grow too strong to be held by the animal nature. *There would be a liberated mind escaping from ignorance into light, aware of its affiliation to Supermind, a natural agent of Supermind and capable of bringing down the supramental influence into the lower reaches of being,* a creator in the light, a discoverer in the depths, an illuminant in the darkness, helping perhaps to penetrate even the Inconscient with the rays of Superconscience. There would be *a new mental being* not only capable of standing enlightened in the radiance of Supermind but able to climb consciously towards it and into it, training life and body to reflect and hold something of the supramental light, power and bliss, aspiring to release the secret divinity into self-finding and self-fulfilment and self-poise, aspiring towards the ascension to the divine consciousness, able to receive and bear the descent of the divine light and power, fitting itself to be a vessel of the divine Life."[18]

The last sentence clearly describes the transitional being, "able to receive and bear the descent of the divine light and power", as a necessary stage between the human and the supramental being in order to make the advent of the latter possible.

"A new humanity would then be a race of mental beings on the earth and in the earthly body", reads the beginning of the sixth article, "but delivered from its present conditions in the reign of the cosmic Ignorance so far as to be possessed of a

---

18. Sri Aurobindo: *Essays in Philosophy and Yoga,* p. 577 (emphasis added).

4. A First Sketch of Supermanhood

perfected mind, *a mind of light, which could even be a subordinate action of the Supermind or Truth-consciousness,* and in any case capable of the full possibilities of mind acting as a recipient of that truth and at least a secondary action of it in thought and life. It could even be a part of what could be described as a divine life upon earth and at least the beginnings of an evolution in the Knowledge and no longer predominantly in the Ignorance."[19] Thus begins the sixth article.

In the seventh article, entitled *The Mind of Light*, Sri Aurobindo takes up again the central theme of the series: "A new humanity means for us the appearance, the development of a type or race of mental beings whose principle of mentality would be no longer a mind in the Ignorance seeking for knowledge but, even in its knowledge bound to the Ignorance, a seeker after Light but not an inhabitant of the Light, not yet a perfected instrument, truth-conscious and delivered out of the Ignorance. Instead, it would be possessed already of what could be called *a mind of Light, a mind capable of living in the truth, capable of being truth-conscious and manifesting in its life a direct in place of an indirect knowledge.*

"Its mentality would be an instrument of the Light and no longer of the Ignorance. At its highest it would be capable of passing into the Supermind *and from the new race would be recruited the race of supramental beings* who would appear as the leaders of the evolution in earth-nature. Even, the highest manifestations of a mind of Light would be an instrumentality of the Supermind, a part of or a projection from it, a stepping beyond humanity into the superhumanity of the supramental principle. Above all, its possession would enable the human being to rise beyond into those highest powers of the mind in its self-exceedings which intervene between our mentality and Supermind and can be regarded as steps leading towards the greater and more luminous principle [i.e. Supermind]."[20]

The highest "powers of the mind" in the last sentence are the same as the aforementioned "powers of the nature still

---
19. Sri Aurobindo: *Essays in Philosophy and Yoga,* p. 578 (emphasis added).
20. Ibid., p. 585 (emphasis added).

belonging to the mental region which are yet potentialities of a growing gnosis lifted beyond our human mentality". "In this *inevitable* ascent the mind of Light is a gradation, an inevitable stage", writes Sri Aurobindo. "As an evolving principle it will mark a stage in the human ascent and evolve *a new type of human being;* this development must carry in it *an ascending gradation of its own powers and types of an ascending humanity* which will embody more and more the turn towards spirituality, capacity for Light, a climb towards a divinised manhood and the divine life."[21] It should be noted that Sri Aurobindo no longer uses the conditional mode in his presentation of "a new type of human being", but that he repeats the word "inevitable", one of his key words when discoursing on the continuation of the earthly evolution and the appearance of a supramental being on the Earth. In the course of this series of articles the language has gradually become more affirmative.

He goes on to say that the embodiment of the Mind of Light will proceed in two stages. "In each of these stages it will define its own grades and manifest the order of its beings who will embody it and give to it a realised life. Thus there will be built up, first, even in the Ignorance itself, the possibility of a human ascent towards a divine living; then there will be, by the illumination of this mind of Light in the greater realisation of what may be called a gnostic mentality, *in a transformation of the human being, even before the Supermind is reached,* even in the earth-consciousness and in a humanity transformed, an illumined divine life."[22] "Supermind and Mind of Light" is the title of the last article; it was published in the *Bulletin* of November 1950 and must have been written one or two months earlier. Here we get the full definition of the Mind of Light. "The Mind of Light is a subordinate action of Supermind, dependent upon it even when not apparently springing directly from it ... In the Mind of Light when it becomes full-orbed this character of the Truth reveals itself, though in a garb that is transparent even when it seems to cover: for this too is a truth-consciousness

---
21. Ibid., p. 587 (emphasis added).
22. Ibid., (emphasis added).

4. A First Sketch of Supermanhood

and a self-power of knowledge. This too proceeds from the Supermind and depends upon it even though it is limited and subordinate.

"What we have called specifically the Mind of Light is indeed the last in a series of descending planes of consciousness in which the Supermind veils itself by a self-chosen limitation or modification of its self-manifesting activities, but its essential character remains the same: there is in it an action of light, of truth, of knowledge in which inconscience, ignorance and error claim no place. It proceeds from knowledge to knowledge; we have not yet crossed over the borders of the truth-consciousness into ignorance."[23]

On 5 December Sri Aurobindo left his body as the outer consequence of a strange uraemic coma from which, visibly by an act of highest yogic mastery, he time and again rose up regaining full waking consciousness. He was entering death consciously because the Law the Creator had imposed upon Himself demanded this unprecedented "strategic" sacrifice. The yogic master-act was possible because the Avatar, complete this time, double-poled, had incarnated in two bodies. The Mother remained, so it had been decided. What her acceptance of staying in the body meant can be (partly) comprehended from the conversations that constitute *Mother's Agenda*.

There she stood, the Mother, when the doctors had declared that Sri Aurobindo was "dead". "She stood there, near the feet of Sri Aurobindo: her hair had been undressed and was flowing about her shoulders", Dr Prabhat Sanyal remembered. "With a piercing gaze she stood there",[24] for a long, long time. This was when the Mother received the Mind of Light from Sri Aurobindo into the cells of her body. "As soon as Sri Aurobindo withdrew from his body, what he has called the Mind of Light got realised in me", the Mother afterwards told K.D. Sethna. "The Supermind had descended long ago – very long ago – into the mind and even into the vital [of Sri Aurobindo and herself]; it was working in the physical also but indirectly through those

---
23. Sri Aurobindo: *Essays in Philosophy and Yoga*, pp. 588-89.
24. Prabhat Sanyal: *A Call from Pondicherry*, p. 4.

intermediaries. The question was about the direct action of the Supermind in the physical. Sri Aurobindo said it could be possible only if the physical mind received the supramental light: the physical mind was the instrument for direct action upon the most material. This physical mind receiving the supramental light Sri Aurobindo called the Mind of Light."[25]

These words of the Mother need some explanation that will be given further on. They are quoted here because they serve to highlight the significance of that moment – and because they confirm, as mooted above, that in his last series of articles Sri Aurobindo made known something that he had first experienced and realised himself. The import of the series of dictated articles, later on published under the title *The Supramental Manifestation upon Earth*, cannot be overestimated. But in the Aurobindonian literature it has hardly been taken note of.

The Levels Above the Rational Mind (1)

"There are powers of the nature still belonging to the mental region which are yet potentialities of a growing gnosis lifted beyond our human mentality and partaking of the light and power of the Divine[,] and an ascent through these planes [and] a descent of them into the mental being might seem to be *the natural evolutionary course*." When these words of Sri Aurobindo were quoted in the beginning of the present chapter, we promised to clarify them to some extent. For they refer to an important range of gradations of being that is little known because it has barely been explored before. Now that the descent of Supermind and the realisation of one or more kinds of intermediary beings between the human and the supramental being was being attempted, this range of gradations became the focus of the *Yoga* of Sri Aurobindo and the Mother.

Both of them had become thoroughly knowledgeable about those higher, spiritual realms during their yogic explorations and experiments. All related data indicate that Sri Aurobindo

---

25. *Words of the Mother,* CWM 13, pp. 63-64.

4. A First Sketch of Supermanhood

and the Mother realised the supramentalisation of the Mind around 1920 and that of the Vital soon afterwards. (This was the time that, according to witnesses, their physical aspects changed so much.) Sri Aurobindo more than once underlines that all gradations are closely connected; therefore, if they personally had realised the Supermind on those levels, they must have realised the intermediate gradations too.

The apparent gap between the human and the supramental being, between the human mind and the Supermind, is enormous. This apparent gap is the cause of "the error to make an unbridgeable gulf between God and man, Brahman and the world".[26] This error resulted in the various conceptions of a supracosmic God, separated from His manifestation or creation. The gap seems to be there because normally to the human being, and therefore to the earthly evolution until now, rational mind is the highest attainment. But the gradations of being run all the way from the Pure Absolute down to the Inconscient. "For the whole of being is a connected totality and there is in it no abrupt passage from the principle of Truth and Light into their opposite ... The depths are linked to the heights and the Law of the one Truth creates and works everywhere."[27] This is the same as saying that there is no gap, hiatus, discontinuity or lacuna anywhere, and that the supposed gap between mind and Supermind is nothing but the consequence of a lack of human spiritual experience.

Let us recall, for clarity's sake, the main rungs of the ladder of being, covering the whole of existence. In the "upper hemisphere" there is Existence, Consciousness-Force, Bliss, and Supermind; in the "lower hemisphere" there is Mind, Life and Matter. Supermind is the manifesting aspect of the Absolute. It is a Truth-Consciousness, a Unity-Consciousness, it is the Brahman with attributes that are usually ascribed to God. We should never forget that every consciousness is also a being. Supermind contains and manifests the Absolute in its

---

26. Sri Aurobindo: *The Life Divine,* p. 131.
27. Sri Aurobindo: *Essays in Philosophy and Yoga,* p. 591. One is here reminded of the basic hermetic principle: "as above so below".

plenitude. And everything manifested, in the upper as well as in the lower hemisphere, *is* the Absolute and could not exist if it were not directly, in its essence, supported by Supermind which is omnipotent and therefore also possesses the power of self-limitation.

The upper and the lower hemisphere are separated by "a golden lid", in some traditions called "the Gate of the Sun", through which no ordinary mortal can pass with the hope of returning. It is on this dividing line or rather in this dividing zone above Mind and below Supermind, that we find the four "spiritual" levels which play such an important part in the subject that concerns us. They are, in descending order and as named by Sri Aurobindo: Overmind, Intuition, Illumined Mind and Higher Mind. Together they make up a region which contains the possible gradations of consciousness of the transitional beings whom Sri Aurobindo called "the new humanity".

Overmind (which is the level of the worlds of the gods), Intuition, Illumined Mind and Higher Mind still exist in the Light of the Supermind, they are, in that order, so to say its increasingly diluted extensions. "... There is an increasing self-limitation [of Supermind] which begins even with Overmind: Overmind is separated by only a luminous border from the full light and power of the supramental Truth and it still commands direct access to all that Supermind can give it." Every overmental Being, or God, represents the Supreme and therefore all the other gods. "There is further limitation or change of characteristic action at each step downwards from Overmind to Intuition, from Intuition to Illumined Mind, from Illumined Mind to what I have called the Higher Mind", writes Sri Aurobindo.[28]

The Absolute is Light, the Inconscient is darkness. Light and darkness in this case are much more than poetic epithets, they are realities. The substances of the Absolute, and therefore of the upper hemisphere, are Light in all its modulations, variations, and powers. The substances of the Inconscient, and therefore of the lower hemisphere, are darkness.

---

28. Sri Aurobindo: *Essays in Philosophy and Yoga*, pp. 589-90.

4. A First Sketch of Supermanhood

Overmind, Intuition, Illumined Mind and Higher Mind are modulations of the Light of the upper hemisphere, while actually belonging to the lower hemisphere. "Thus there is a succession of ranges of consciousness which we can speak of as Mind but which belongs practically to the higher hemisphere, although in their ontological station they are within the domain of the lower hemisphere."[29] A metaphor may make clear what many a reader may find confusing. If the Supermind is symbolised by a Sun and the lower hemisphere by an ocean, then the rays of the sun penetrate the surface of the ocean and illumine its highest layers till the water gradually becomes darker and finally completely dark. According to Sri Aurobindo the highest levels of the lower hemisphere, the layers above the mind, still receive the light of the supramental Sun although they actually belong to the ocean of fragmentation and darkness that is the lower hemisphere.

The following quotation from Sri Aurobindo gives a hint of the importance of these transitional levels: "In the transformation by the Higher Mind the spiritual sage and thinker would find his total and dynamic fulfilment; in the transformation by the Illumined Mind there would be a similar fulfilment for the seer, the illumined mystic, those in whom the soul lives in vision and in a direct sense and experience: for it is from these higher sources that they receive their light and to rise into that light and live there would be their ascension to their native empire."[30] In other words, the lowest two of these four ranges represent the highest ranges of consciousness humanity had access to until now. ("Intuition" in this context means something very different from the mostly untrustworthy, because deformed, intuitive flashes that sometimes visit us: it is a direct though not complete revelation of the Supermind.)

---

29. Ibid., p. 591.
30. Sri Aurobindo: *The Life Divine,* p. 946.

Mind

To gain a clearer insight into the role and significance of the spiritual levels,[31] we will take a brief look at Mind itself, as described by Sri Aurobindo. It is no exaggeration to assert that Mind is the main instrument as well as the object of philosophical thought in the West. A real understanding of Mind should be part of a real understanding of the human being as a whole, but one does not have to delve very deeply into Western philosophy to find out that confusion on this topic is rife. The greatest authorities contradict each other with the greatest authority. The point is that as long as the West keeps exploring the surfaces of existence, it cannot find out the fundamentals of things. Sri Aurobindo and the Mother's understanding represents the findings of old, in-depth and patiently researched traditions, perfected by their own experience which went beyond all former experience.

Their writings and sayings on the subject of Mind are extensive. The following quotes from *The Life Divine* give a first notion.

- "Mind is not a faculty of knowledge nor an instrument of omniscience; it is a faculty for the seeking of knowledge, for expressing as much as it can gain of it in certain forms of a relative thought and for using it towards certain capacities of action. Even when it finds, it does not possess; it only keeps a certain fund of current coin of Truth – not Truth itself – in the bank of Memory to draw upon according to its needs. For Mind is that which does not know, which tries to know and which never knows except as in a glass darkly. It is the power which interprets truth of universal existence for the practical uses of a certain order of things; it is not the

---

31. Overmind, Intuition, Illumined Mind and Higher Mind are of course supra-mental. But to avoid confusion with Supermind, which is also named "the Supramental" and which is designated by the adjective "supramental", we will call them, in agreement with Sri Aurobindo's terminology, "spiritual".

4. A First Sketch of Supermanhood

power which knows and guides that existence and therefore it cannot be the power which created or manifested it."[32]

- "Its function [of Mind] is to cut something vaguely from the unknown Thing in itself and call this measurement or delimitation of it the whole, and again to analyse the whole into its parts which it regards as separate mental objects. It is only the parts and accidents that the Mind can see definitely and, after its own fashion, know. Of the whole its only definite idea is an assemblage of parts or a totality of properties and accidents. The whole not seen as a part of something else or in its own parts, properties and accidents is to the mind no more than a vague perception; only when it is analysed and put by itself as separate constituted object, a totality in a larger totality, can Mind say to itself, 'This now I know.' And really it does not know. It knows only its own analysis of the object and the idea it has formed of it by a synthesis of the separate parts and properties that it has seen. There its characteristic power, its sure function ceases, and if we would have a greater, a profounder and a real knowledge, – a knowledge and not an intense but formless sentiment such as comes sometimes to certain deep but inarticulate parts of our mentality, – Mind has to make room for another consciousness which will fulfil Mind by transcending it or reverse and so rectify its operations after leaping beyond it: the summit of mental knowledge is only a vaulting-board from which the leap can be taken. The utmost mission of Mind is to train our obscure consciousness which has emerged out of the dark prison of Matter, to enlighten its blind instincts, random intuitions, vague perceptions till it shall become capable of this greater light and this higher ascension. Mind is a passage, not a culmination."[33]

- "Mind can conceive with precision divisions as real; it can conceive a synthetic totality or the finite extending itself

---
32. Sri Aurobindo: *The Life Divine*, pp. 118.
33. Ibid., p. 128.

indefinitely; it can grasp aggregates of divided things and the samenesses underlying them; but the ultimate unity and absolute infinity are to its conscience of things abstract notions and unseizable quantities, not something that is real to its grasp, much less something that is alone real. Here is therefore the very opposite term to the Unitarian consciousness ..."[34]

- "But if we suppose an infinite Mind which would be free from our limitations, that at least might well be the creator of the universe? But such a Mind would be something quite different from the definition of mind as we know it: it would be something beyond mentality; it would be the supramental Truth. An infinite Mind constituted in the terms of mentality as we know it could only create an infinite chaos, a vast clash of chance, accident, vicissitude wandering towards an indeterminate end after which it would be always tentatively groping and aspiring. An infinite, omniscient, omnipotent Mind would not be mind at all, but supramental knowledge."[35]

In the series of articles Sri Aurobindo wrote for the *Bulletin*, he also characterises Mind. "... Mind is not a power of whole knowledge and only when it begins to pass beyond itself a power of direct knowledge: it receives rays from the truth but does not live in the sun; it sees as through glasses and its knowledge is coloured by its instruments, it cannot see with the naked eye or look straight at the sun ... It is a power for creation, but either tentative and uncertain and succeeding by good chance or the favour of circumstance, or else if assured by some force of practical ability or genius, subject to flaw or pent within inescapable limits. Its highest knowledge is often abstract, lacking in a concrete grasp; it has to use expedients and unsure means of arrival, to rely upon reasoning, argumentation and debate, inferences, divinations, set methods of inductive or deductive logic, succeeding only if it is given correct and complete data

---
34. Ibid., p. 127.
35. Ibid.

4. A First Sketch of Supermanhood

and even then liable to reach on the same data different results and varying consequences ..."[36]

Mind "is used by the Supermind principally for the work of differentiation which is necessary if there is to be a creation and a universe" – if there are to be separate, (apparently) independently existing beings and things. "In the Supermind itself, in all its creation there is this differentiating power, the manifestation of the One in the Many and the Many in the One; but the One is never forgotten or lost in its multiplicity which always consciously depends upon and never takes precedence over the eternal oneness. In the mind, on the contrary, the differentiation, the multiplicity does take precedence and the conscious sense of the universal oneness is lost and the separated unit seems to exist for itself and by itself as a sufficient self-conscious integer or in inanimate objects as the inconscient integer."[37]

This means that Mind has been made into the instrument of a practical (apparent) division of the One and its Oneness. In the descending order this lowest gradation of the Light had to plunge into the darkness of the Inconscient, and rise out of it in the ascending order for its characteristic embodiment in our species of human beings. Mind is a darkened substance of Light, necessary in the scheme of things to make the existence of "the inconscient or self-conscious integers" possible. It always vaguely remembers the fundamental Unity at its base; therefore it cannot but persistently try to recover that Unity, which is the clouded Sun behind all human strivings. It is that Sun, that Unity, the Supermind which upholds all existing things, even when they *apparently* seem to be separated or self-existent. For all exists in That, all is Brahman.

---

36. Sri Aurobindo: *Essays in Philosophy and Yoga*, p. 575.
37. Sri Aurobindo: *Essays in Philosophy and Yoga*, pp. 572-73. The dictionary says that "integer" means "an individual entity or whole unit".

The Levels Above the Rational Mind (2)

As we are now a bit better acquainted with Mind, the pride of our species, we may return to the spiritual levels for a closer look, for until now they have been defined only in a general, abstract way. Sri Aurobindo has described these four levels – Higher Mind, Illumined Mind, Intuition, and Overmind – for the very first time in the history of human thought and spirituality extensively in *The Life Divine*.[38] His description covers many pages and we will have again to content ourselves with a few key passages. It is important to remember that these are not philosophical abstractions, but condensed and highly expressive wordings of spiritual experiences.

In "the natural configuration of the stair of ascent" there are "many steps, for it is an incessant gradation and there is no gap anywhere", writes Sri Aurobindo, "but from the point of view of the ascent of consciousness from our mind upwards, through a rising series of dynamic powers by which it can sublimate itself, the gradation can be resolved into a stairway of four main ascents, each with its high level of fulfilment. These gradations may be summarily described as a series of sublimations of the consciousness through Higher Mind, Illumined Mind and Intuition into Overmind and beyond it ... All these degrees are gnostic [i.e. supramental] in their principle and power ...

"In themselves these grades are grades of energy-substance of the Spirit: for it must not be supposed, because we distinguish them according to their leading character, means and potency of knowledge, that they are merely a method or way of knowing or a faculty or power of cognition; they are domains of being, grades of the substance and energy of the spiritual being, fields of existence which are each a level of the universal

---

38. Sri Aurobindo is reported to have told some disciples in 1938: "It was Vivekananda who, when he used to come to me during meditation in Alipore Jail, showed me the Intuitive Plane. For a month or so he gave instructions about Intuition. Then afterwards I began to see the still higher planes." (Nirodbaran: *Talks with Sri Aurobindo* I, p. 53) Sri Aurobindo was imprisoned in Alipore Jail from May 1908 till May 1909; Swami Vivekananda had died in 1902.

4. A First Sketch of Supermanhood

Consciousness-Force constituting and organising itself into a higher status. When the powers of any grade descend completely into us, it is not only our thought and knowledge that are affected, – the substance and very grain of our being and consciousness, all its states and activities are touched and penetrated and can be remoulded and wholly transmuted. Each stage of this ascent is therefore a general, if not a total, conversion of the being into a new light and power of a greater existence."[39]

Higher Mind: "Our first decisive step out of our human intelligence, our normal mentality, is an ascent into a higher Mind, a mind no longer of mingled light and obscurity or half-light, but a large clarity of the Spirit. Its basic substance is a Unitarian sense of being with a powerful multiple dynamisation capable of the formation of a multitude of aspects of knowledge, ways of action, forms and significances of becoming, of all of which there is a spontaneous inherent knowledge. It is therefore a power that has proceeded from the Overmind, – but with the Supermind as its ulterior origin, – as all these greater powers have proceeded: but its special character, its activity of consciousness are dominated by Thought; it is a luminous thought-mind, a mind of Spirit-born conceptual knowledge.

"An all-awareness emerging from the original identity, carrying the truths the identity held in itself, conceiving swiftly, victoriously, multitudinously, formulating and by self-power of the Idea effectually realising its conceptions, is the character of this greater mind of knowledge. This kind of cognition is the last that emerges [in the descending order] from the original spiritual identity before the initiation of a separative knowledge, base of the Ignorance; it is therefore the first [in the ascending order] that meets us when we rise from conceptive and ratiocinative mind, our best organised knowledge-power of the Ignorance, into the realms of the Spirit; it is, indeed, the spiritual parent of our conceptive mental ideation ..."[40]

Illumined Mind: Illumined Mind is "a Mind no longer of higher Thought, but of spiritual light. Here the clarity of

---
39. Sri Aurobindo: *The Life Divine,* pp. 937-38.
40. Sri Aurobindo: *The Life Divine,* pp. 939-40.

the spiritual intelligence, its tranquil daylight, gives place or subordinates itself to an intense lustre, a splendour and illumination of the Spirit: a play of lightnings of spiritual truth and power breaks from above into the consciousness and adds to the calm and wide enlightenment and the vast descent of peace which characterise or accompany the action of the larger conceptual-spiritual principle, a fiery ardour of realisation and a rapturous ecstasy of knowledge.

"A downpour of inwardly visible Light very usually envelops this action; for it must be noted that, contrary to our ordinary conceptions, light is not primarily a material creation and the sense of vision of light accompanying the inner illumination is not merely a subjective visual image or a symbolic phenomenon: light is primarily a spiritual manifestation of the Divine Reality illuminative and creative; material light is a subsequent representation or conversion of it into Matter for the purposes of the material Energy. There is also in this descent [of the Illumined Mind] the arrival of a greater dynamic, a golden drive, a luminous 'enthousiasmos' of inner force and power which replaces the comparatively slow and deliberate process of the Higher Mind by a swift, sometimes a vehement, almost a violent impetus of rapid transformation.

"The Illumined Mind does not work primarily by thought but by vision; thought is here only a subordinate movement expressive of sight ..."[41]

Intuition: "Intuition is a power of consciousness nearer and more intimate to the original knowledge of identity; for it is always something that leaps out direct from a concealed identity. It is when the consciousness of the subject meets with the consciousness in the object, penetrates it and sees, feels or vibrates with the truth of what it contacts, that the intuition leaps out like a spark or lightning-flash from the shock of the meeting; or when the consciousness, even without any such meeting, looks into itself and feels directly and intimately the truth or the truths that are there or so contacts the hidden forces behind appearances, then also there is the outbreak of

---

41. Ibid., p. 944.

4. A First Sketch of Supermanhood

an intuitive light; or, again, when the consciousness meets the Supreme Reality or the spiritual reality of things and beings and has a contactual union with it, then the spark, the flash or the blaze of intimate truth-perception is lit in its depths. This close perception is more than sight, more than conception: it is the result of a penetrating and revealing touch which carries in it sight and conception as part of itself or as its natural consequence. A concealed or slumbering identity, not yet recovering itself, still remembers or conveys by the intuition its own contents and the intimacy of its self-feeling and self-vision of things, its light of truth, its overwhelming and automatic certitude ...

"Intuition is always an edge or ray or outleap of a superior light; it is in us a projecting blade, edge or point of a far-off Supermind light entering into and modified by some intermediate truth-mind substance above us and, so modified, again entering into and very much blinded by our ordinary or ignorant mind-substance; but on that higher level to which it is native its light is unmixed and therefore entirely and purely veridical, and its rays are not separated but connected or massed together in a play of waves of what might almost be called in the Sanskrit poetic figure a sea or mass of 'stable lightnings'."[42]

Overmind: "The next step of the ascent brings us to the Overmind; the intuitional change can only be an introduction to this higher spiritual overture. But we have seen that the Overmind, even when it is selective and not total in its action, is still a power of cosmic consciousness, a principle of global knowledge which carries in it a delegated light from the supramental Gnosis. It is, therefore, only by an opening into the cosmic consciousness that the overmind ascent and descent can be made wholly possible: a high and intense individual opening upwards is not sufficient, – to that vertical ascent towards summit Light there must be added a vast horizontal expansion of the consciousness into some totality of the Spirit. At the least, the inner being must already have replaced by its deeper and wider awareness the surface mind and its limited outlook

---
42. Sri Aurobindo: *The Life Divine*, pp. 946-47.

and learned to live in a large universality; for otherwise the overmind view of things and the overmind dynamism will have no room to move in and effectuate its dynamic operations.

"When the Overmind descends, the predominance of the centralising ego-sense is entirely subordinated, lost in largeness of being and finally abolished; a wide cosmic perception and feeling of a boundless universal self and movement replaces it: many motions that were formerly egocentric may still continue, but they occur as currents or ripples in the cosmic wideness.

Thought, for the most part, no longer seems to originate individually in the body or the person but manifests from above or comes in upon the cosmic mind-waves: all inner individual sight or intelligence of things is now a revelation or illumination of what is seen or comprehended, but the source of the revelation is not in one's separate self but in the universal knowledge; the feelings, emotions, sensations are similarly felt as waves from the same cosmic immensity breaking upon the subtle and the gross body and responded to in kind by the individual centre of the universality; for the body is only a small support or even less, a point of relation, for the action of a vast cosmic instrumentation.

"In this boundless largeness, not only the separate ego but all sense of individuality, even of a subordinated or instrumental individuality, may entirely disappear; the cosmic existence, the cosmic consciousness, the cosmic delight, the play of cosmic forces are alone left: if the delight or the centre of Force is felt in what was the personal mind, life or body, it is not with a sense of personality but as a field of manifestation, and this sense of the delight or of the action of Force is not confined to the person or the body but can be felt at all points in an unlimited consciousness of unity which pervades everywhere."[43]

To the above should be added by way of completion and comment the following points.

The Soul: What we have not yet read about is the essence, cause and support of our incarnation: the soul. It is, once again, no exaggeration to state that the confusion about the soul in

---

43. Sri Aurobindo: *The Life Divine*, pp. 950-51.

the religious and spiritual literature is dumbfounding, and not only in Christianity. Sri Aurobindo and the Mother's view on this topic, as on all others, is on the contrary clear, complete, and a reliable basis for spiritual practice.

"*The soul*, representative of the central being, is a spark of the Divine supporting all individual existence in Nature; *the psychic being* is a conscious form of that soul growing in the evolution – in the persistent process that develops first life in Matter, mind in life, until finally mind can develop into overmind and overmind into the supramental Truth. *The soul supports the nature in its evolution through these grades, but is itself not any of these things* ..."[44]

"The soul or psyche is immutable only in the sense that it contains all the possibilities of the Divine within it, but it has to evolve them and in its evolution assumes the form of a developing psychic individual [the psychic being] evolving in the manifestation the individual Prakriti [Nature] and taking part in the evolution. It is the spark of the Divine Fire that grows behind the mind, vital and physical by means of the psychic being until it is able to transform the Prakriti of Ignorance into a Prakriti of Knowledge. This evolving psychic being is not therefore at any time all that the soul or essential psychic existence bears within it; it temporalises and individualises what is eternal in potentiality, transcendent in essence, in this projection of the spirit.

"The central being *[jivatman]* is the being which presides over the different births one after the other, but is itself unborn, for it does not descend into the being but is above it – it holds together the mental, vital and physical being and all the various parts of the personality and it controls the life either through the mental being and the mental thought and will or through the psychic *[antaratman]*, whichever may happen to be the most in front or most powerful in nature ...

"The psychic is not above but behind – its seat is behind the

---

44. This corrects the common error, also found in contemporary writings about the Great Chain of Being, which locates the soul as a gradation within the grand scale, usually just above the mind.

heart, its power is not knowledge but an essential or spiritual feeling – it has the clearest sense of the Truth and a sort of inherent perception of it which is of the nature of soul-perception and soul-feeling. It is our inmost being and supports all the others, mental, vital, physical, but it is also much veiled by them as an influence rather than by its sovereign right of direct action; its direct action becomes normal and preponderant only at a high stage of development or by yoga ..."[45]

Let us add the following clarifications. "The Jivatma, spark-soul [Antaratma] and psychic being are three different forms of the same reality and they must not be mixed together, as that confuses the clearness of the inner experience." Secondly: "The soul is a spark of the Divine in the heart of the living creatures of Nature ... This spark of Divinity is there in all terrestrial living beings from the earth's highest to its lowest creatures." But it is only in humans that it becomes individualised and is given shape, as it were, by a psychic being. Thirdly: "The psychic being is a spiritual personality put forward by the soul in its evolution; its growth marks the stage which the spiritual evolution of the individual has reached and its immediate possibilities for the future. It stands behind the mental, the vital, the physical nature, grows by their experiences, carries the consciousness from life to life."[46]

The realisation of the psychic being, i.e. the state of becoming concretely aware of it and living in it, is the first important aim and *siddhi* of the Integral Yoga. The second is the realisation of the spiritual levels which are the main focus of our attention in this chapter, and the third the realisation of the Supermind and the transformation of the body.

Reality of the Spirit: As was pointed out before, it is a common misconception that matter is concrete and dense, while the Spirit gradually becomes less substantial, more ethereal on every higher level. On the contrary, Sri Aurobindo puts it like this: "Consciousness, as we *descend* the scale, becomes more and more diminished and diluted, – dense indeed by its

---
45. Sri Aurobindo: *Letters on Yoga*, p. 267 ff. (emphasis added).
46. Ibid., pp. 280-81.

coarser crudity, but while that crudity of consistence compacts the stuff of Ignorance, it admits less and less the substance of light; it becomes thin in pure substance of consciousness and reduced in power of consciousness, thin in light, thin and weak in capacity of delight; it has to resort to a grosser thickness of its diminished stuff and to a strenuous output of its obscurer force to arrive at anything, but this strenuousness of effort and labour is a sign not of strength but of weakness.

"As we *ascend*, on the contrary, a finer but far stronger and more truly and spiritually concrete substance emerges, a greater luminosity and potent stuff of consciousness, a subtler, sweeter, purer and more powerfully ecstatic energy of delight."[47] Again, Sri Aurobindo is clearly relying on his personal spiritual experience. The philosophic masterpiece that is *The Life Divine* is in fact from beginning to end an account of his own experiences.

Interpenetrability. We have enumerated the four spiritual levels, just as we have discerned the other tiers of the Great Chain of Being. To do so is indispensable, but this may also, in part or on the whole, distort our view of the reality. We should never forget that all is One, undivided, and that division is the typical way in which the Mind functions, because otherwise it can have no hold on reality, it cannot comprehend. But "the whole of being is a connected totality and there is in it no abrupt passage from the principle of Truth and Light into their opposite."[48]

"In themselves these grades [i.e. the four spiritual levels] are grades of energy-substance of the Spirit: for it must not be supposed, because we distinguish them according to their leading character, means and potency of knowledge, that they are merely a method or way of knowing or a faculty or power of cognition; they are domains of being, grades of the substance and energy of the spiritual being, fields of existence which are each a level of the universal Consciousness-Force constituting and organising itself into a higher status. *When the powers of any grade descend completely into us, it is not only our thought and*

---

47. Sri Aurobindo: *The Life Divine*, pp. 938-39 (emphasis added).
48. Sri Aurobindo: *Essays in Philosophy and Yoga*, p. 591.

knowledge that are affected, – the substance and very grain of our being and consciousness, all its states and activities are touched and penetrated and can be remoulded and wholly transmuted. Each stage of this ascent is therefore a general, if not a total, conversion of the being into a new light and power of a greater existence."[49]

These words are of immense importance for people who do not have the experience and who are interested in this kind of adventure. For, firstly, they tell us that a realisation of one of the spiritual levels has a direct repercussion on the physical body, on the *adhara*. We will have to come back to this when we learn about the work the Mother did for "the new humanity". For the Mind of Light, which is the consciousness of that new humanity, is part of the spiritual levels, as we shall presently see.

Secondly, these words explain the complex, seemingly chaotic movements of the Integral Yoga. In the previous chapter we quoted Sri Aurobindo's comparison of the Yoga to "an army advancing in columns which annexes new ground" and has to adapt to the situation. On the same occasion he writes: "But evolutionary Nature is not a logical series of separate segments; it is a totality of ascending powers of being which interpenetrate and dovetail and exercise in their action on each other a power of mutual modification. When the higher descends into the lower consciousness, it alters the lower but is also modified and diminished by it; when the lower ascends, it is sublimated but at the same time qualifies the sublimating substance and power. This interaction creates an abundant number of different intermediate and interlocked degrees of the force and consciousness of being, but it also makes it difficult to bring about a complete integration of all the powers under the full control of any one power.

"For this reason *there is not actually a series of simple clear-cut and successive stages in the individual's evolution; there is instead a complexity and a partly determinate, partly confused comprehensiveness of the movement.* The soul may still be described as a traveller and climber who presses towards his high goal step by step, each of which he has to build up as an integer but must

---
49. Sri Aurobindo: *The Life Divine,* p. 938 (emphasis added).

frequently redescend in order to rebuild and make sure of the supporting stair so that it may not crumble beneath him: but the evolution of the whole consciousness has rather the movement of an ascending ocean of Nature; it can be compared to a tide or a mounting flux, the leading fringe of which touches the higher degrees of a cliff or hill while the rest is still below. At each stage the higher parts of the nature may be provisionally but incompletely organised in the new consciousness while the lower are in a state of flux or formation, partly moving in the old way though influenced and beginning to change, partly belonging to the new kind but still imperfectly achieved and not yet firm in the change."[50]

The Necessity of Transitional Beings

The announcement in *The Supramental Manifestation upon Earth* of the creation of "a new humanity", of beings or kinds of beings in between the human and the supramental species, was a new development in the supramental Yoga, in the enormously concentrated effort of Sri Aurobindo and the Mother to give a totally new turn to evolution within the span of a single lifetime. But was such a development completely unforeseen? The gap between Mind and Supermind being so large, how could it reasonably be supposed that it could be bridged without something in between? "For the gulf between Mind and Supermind has to be bridged, the closed passages opened and roads of ascent and descent created where there is now a void and a silence",[51] wrote Sri Aurobindo in the *Arya,* some thirty years before his articles were composed for the *Bulletin*. To put the progress of the Yoga from the *Arya* articles onward into perspective, we shall simply quote some relevant paragraphs from his early writings.

- "If a spiritual unfolding on earth is the hidden truth of our

---

50. Sri Aurobindo: *The Life Divine,* pp. 955-56 (emphasis added).
51. Ibid., p. 891.

birth into Matter, if it is fundamentally an evolution of consciousness that has been taking place in Nature, then man as he is cannot be the last term of that evolution: he is too imperfect an expression of the Spirit, Mind itself a too limited form and instrumentation; Mind is only a middle term of consciousness, the mental being can only be a transitional being. If, then, man is incapable of exceeding mentality, he must be surpassed and Supermind and superman must manifest and take the lead of the creation. *But if his mind is capable of opening to what exceeds it, then there is no reason why man himself should not arrive at Supermind and supermanhood or at least lend his mentality, life and body to an evolution of that greater term of the spirit manifesting in Nature.*"[52]

- "When the gnosis is gained, it can then be turned on the whole nature to divinise the human being. It is impossible to rise into it at once; if that could be done, it would mean a sudden and violent overshooting, a breaking or slipping through the gates of the Sun, *suryasya dvara*, without near possibility of return. *We have to form as a link or a bridge an intuitive or illuminated mind, which is not the direct gnosis, but in which a first derivative body of the gnosis can form.* This illumined mind will first be a mixed power which we shall have to purify of all its mental dependence and mental forms so as to convert all willing and thinking into thought-sight and truth-seeing will by an illumined discrimination, intuition, inspiration, revelation. That will be the final purification of the intelligence and the preparation for the Siddhi of the gnosis."[53]

- "*Even before the gnostic change there can be a beginning* of this fundamental ecstasy of being translated into a manifold beauty and delight. In the mind, it translates into a calm of intense delight of spiritual perception and vision and knowledge, in the heart into a wide or deep or passionate delight of universal union and love and sympathy and the

---

52. Ibid., p. 847 (emphasis added).
53. Sri Aurobindo: *The Synthesis of Yoga,* p. 673 (emphasis added).

4. A First Sketch of Supermanhood

joy of beings and the joy of things. In the will and vital parts it is felt as the energy of delight of a divine life-power in action or a beatitude of the sense perceiving and meeting the One everywhere, perceiving as their normal aesthesis of things a universal beauty and a secret harmony of creation of which our mind can catch only imperfect glimpses or a rare supernormal sense. In the body it reveals itself as an ecstasy pouring into it from the heights of the Spirit and the peace and bliss of a pure and spiritualised physical existence."[54]

- "In the untransformed part of humanity itself there might well arise a new and greater order of mental human beings; *for the directly intuitive or partly intuitivised but not yet gnostic mental being, the directly or partly illumined mental being, the mental being in direct or part communion with the higher-thought plane would emerge:* these would become more and more numerous, more and more evolved and secure in their type, and might even exist as a formed race of higher humanity leading upwards the less evolved in a true fraternity born of the sense of the manifestation of the One Divine in all beings."[55] These words may also be applicable to the levels of humanity, overhumanity and superhumanity that are likely to exist simultaneously in the future.

- "Therefore the individuals who will most help the future of humanity in the new age will be those who will recognise a spiritual evolution as the destiny and therefore the great need of the human being. Even as the animal man has been largely converted into a mentalised and at the top a highly mentalised humanity, so too now or in the future an evolution or conversion – it does not greatly matter which figure we use or what theory we adopt to support it – of the present type of humanity into a spiritualised humanity is the need of the race and surely the intention of Nature; that evolution or conversion will be their ideal and endeavour.

---

54. Sri Aurobindo: *The Life Divine*, p. 991 (emphasis added).
55. Ibid., p. 1012 (emphasis added).

They will be comparatively indifferent to particular belief and form and leave men to resort to the beliefs and forms to which they are naturally drawn. They will only hold as essential the faith in this spiritual conversion, the attempt to live it out and whatever knowledge – the form of opinion into which it is thrown does not so much matter – can be converted into this living. They will especially not make the mistake of thinking that this change can be effected by machinery and outward institutions; they will know and never forget that it has to be lived out by each man inwardly or it can never be made a reality for the kind. They will adopt in its heart of meaning the inward view of the East which bids man seek the secret of his destiny and salvation within; but also they will accept, though with a different turn given to it, the importance which the West rightly attaches to life and to the making the best we know and can attain the general rule of all life."[56]

This selection of quotations is far from exhaustive. Yet it shows convincingly the enormous will of Sri Aurobindo and the Mother to change humanity into something better and higher. The spiritual was never left out of their view and the material was always used as their stepping stone. There is no greater epic than the story of their lives; but its episodes were for the most part unseen, not "in front of the curtain"; and they remain for the most part unknown.

The Mind of Light

Our ordinary human mind is a mind of confusion and darkness; a look into this morning's newspaper will confirm this right away. In the last months of his life Sri Aurobindo announced the coming of a kind of being that would possess a mind of clarity and light.

Let us then at this point of our exposition recall how he

---

56. Sri Aurobindo: *The Human Cycle*, pp. 265-66.

4. A First Sketch of Supermanhood

defined that Mind of Light in the last of his articles for the *Bulletin*.[57] (All emphases are added.)

- "The Mind of Light is *a subordinate action of Supermind,* dependent upon it even when not apparently springing directly from it ..." *(Essays in Philosophy and Yoga,* p. 588)

- "In the Mind of Light when it becomes full-orbed this character of the Truth reveals itself, though in a garb that is transparent even when it seems to cover: for this too is a truth-consciousness and a self-power of knowledge. *This too proceeds from the Supermind and depends upon it even though it is limited and subordinate.* What we have called the Mind of Light is indeed *the last of a series of descending planes of consciousness in which the Supermind veils itself* by a self-chosen limitation or modification of its self-manifesting activities, but its essential character remains the same: there is in it an action of light, of truth, of knowledge in which inconscience, ignorance and error claim no place. It proceeds from knowledge to knowledge; we have not yet crossed over the borders of the truth-consciousness into ignorance." (p. 589) It should be noted that Sri Aurobindo locates the Mind of Light in the descending order of the spiritual levels as "the last of a series of descending planes of consciousness" where the border of the truth-consciousness into the ignorance is not yet crossed. In the inverse order the Mind of Light will be (or is already) the first acquisition by some advanced human beings of the Truth-Consciousness or Supermind in its most "diluted" aspect.

- "There is a further limitation or change of characteristic action [of the supramental consciousness] at each step downwards from Overmind to Intuition, from Intuition to Illumined Mind, from Illumined Mind to what I have called the Higher Mind: the Mind of Light is a transitional passage by which we can pass from Supermind and superhumanity

---

57. The two authors who have been most aware of the importance of the Mind of Light are K.D. Sethna, e.g. in his *The Vison and Work of Sri Aurobindo,* and R.Y. Deshpande, e.g. in *Sri Aurobindo and the New Millennium.*

to an illumined humanity. For the new humanity will be capable of at least *a partly divinised way of seeing and living* because it will live in the light and in knowledge and not in the obscuration of the ignorance." (p. 590) Again Sri Aurobindo is locating "the new humanity" in the descending order. From this passage one might conclude that the character, intensity or degree of the Mind of Light may vary to some degree and that it belongs, generally speaking, to the levels of either Higher or Illumined Mind. We already know that these two levels are the highest attained by mankind until the present in its thinkers, poets,[58] sages, mystics, seers and saints. Now the acquisition of the Mind of Light (1) would no longer be a personal feat but an evolutionary step forward of humankind in many individuals, preparing the advent of the supramental species; (2) it would cause and even require bodily changes necessary to allow for "a partly divinised way of seeing and living".

A Normal Evolutionary Process

Sri Aurobindo wrote as early as in *The Life Divine*: "In a future transformation the character of the evolution, the principle of evolutionary process, although modified, will not fundamentally change but, on a vaster scale and in a liberated movement, royally continue."[59] Palaeontology tells us that there have been intermediary, transitional beings between the primates and *homo sapiens*. The appearance of a "new humanity" of transitional beings would therefore be the normal and necessary

---

58. Sri Aurobindo encouraged the writing of poetry (as well as the practice of other art forms) because his concentration – the striving for inspiration – brings the poet into contact with the spiritual levels above the mind. Several of his disciples were talented poets who sought the guidance and critical appreciation of their Master. The ease with which Sri Aurobindo traced many of their lines to the various spiritual or "overhead" planes from where they originated, is remarkable and a true innovation in literature. See K.D. Sethna's *Overhead Poetry: Poems with Sri Aurobindo's Comments,* and Nirodbaran's *Fifty Poems with Sri Aurobindo's Comments.*
59. Sri Aurobindo: *The Life Divine,* p. 727.

4. A First Sketch of Supermanhood

preamble to the realisation of the supramental being on the Earth. "The advance [i.e. the coming of a new, higher species beyond humanity], however it comes about, will indeed be of the nature of a miracle, as are all such profound changes and immense developments, for they have the appearance of a kind of realised impossibility. But God works all his miracles by an evolution of secret possibilities which have been long prepared, at least in their elements, and in the end by a rapid bringing of all to a head, a throwing together of the elements so that in their fusion they produce a new form and name of things and reveal a new spirit. Often the decisive turn is preceded by an apparent emphasising and raising to their extreme of things which seem the very denial, the most uncompromising opposite of the new principle and the new creation."[60]

"All the facts show that a type can vary within its own specification of nature", wrote Sri Aurobindo, "but there is nothing to show that it can go beyond it. It has not yet been really established that ape-kind developed into man; for it would rather seem that a type resembling the ape, but always characteristic of itself and not of apehood, developed within its own tendencies of nature and became what we know as man, the present human being." This, written around 1920 in the *Arya,* seems to be in agreement with the latest conclusions of evolutionary biology. "It is not even established that inferior races of man developed out of themselves the superior races; those of an inferior organisation and capacity perished, but it has not been shown that they left behind the human races of today as their descendants: but still a development within the type is imaginable."[61]

In the same chapter, Sri Aurobindo returned to the subject: "If the appearance in animal being of a type similar in some respects to the ape-kind but already from the beginning endowed with the elements of humanity was the method of the human evolution, the appearance in the human being of a spiritual type resembling mental-animal humanity but already with the stamp of the spiritual aspiration on it would be the

---
60. Sri Aurobindo: *The Human Cycle,* p. 183.
61. Sri Aurobindo: *The Life Divine,* p. 829.

obvious method of Nature for the evolutionary production of the spiritual and supramental being."[62] Towards the end of his life he discovered or communicated the knowledge for the first time: that "a spiritual type resembling mental-animal humanity" was to become an evolutionary fact, but in place of a "spiritual aspiration" it would be endowed with the first lights of the Supermind.

One of the main problems of the avataric effort was that the foundations of the future had to be secured within the span of a human lifetime. This meant that a new evolutionary turn and acceleration, which normally takes thousands and more often millions of years, had to be initiated within less than a century.

"My difficulty is", wrote Sri Aurobindo to a disciple in 1933, "that you all seem to expect a kind of miraculous fairy-tale change and do not realise that it is a rapid and concentrated evolution which is the aim of my Sadhana [and the Mother's] and that there must be a process for it, a working of the higher in the lower and a dealing with all the necessary intervals – not a sudden feat of creation by which everything is done on a given date. It is a supramental but not an irrational process. What is to be done will happen – perhaps with a rush even – but in a workmanlike way and not according to Faerie."[63] And he wrote to another disciple: "But in its nature the Descent [of the Supermind] is not something arbitrary and miraculous but a rapid evolutionary process compressed into a few years. That cannot be done in the whole world at a time, but it is done like all such processes, first through selected Adharas and then on a wider scale. We have to do it through ourselves [Sri Aurobindo meant himself and the Mother] first and through the circle of Sadhaks gathered around us in the terrestrial consciousness as typified there. If a few open, that is sufficient for the process to be possible."[64] At the time this last passage was written, the expectation was still of a direct descent of the Supermind, to be concretised by an appearance on earth of the supramental

---

62. Ibid., p. 842.
63. Sri Aurobindo: *On Himself,* p. 147.
64. Ibid., p. 471.

4. A First Sketch of Supermanhood

being. But now, at this point in our story, it became obvious that a transitional kind of being in the evolutionary scale was required.

5.
Overman

> *The Truth is not linear but global; it is not successive but simultaneous. Therefore it cannot be expressed in words: it has to be lived.*[1]
>
> – the Mother

In December 1972, less than a year before she would lay down her body, the Mother thought back to that crucial moment on 5 December 1950: the passing of Sri Aurobindo. "He had gathered in his body much supramental Force and as soon as he left ... You see, he was lying on his bed, I stood near him, and in a way altogether concrete – so concrete, I felt it so strongly that I thought it could be seen – all the supramental Force that was in him passed from his body into mine. And I felt the friction of the passage. It was extraordinary. It was an extraordinary experience. For a long time, a long time, like this *(gesture indicating the passage of the Force into her body)*. I was standing beside his bed and that came into my body. Almost a sensation – it was a material sensation. For a long time. And that is all I know."[2]

Sri Aurobindo's departure had been a shattering blow to her, "an annihilation". They, the double-poled Avatar, were after all one and the same consciousness – one and the same supernal Consciousness that is Love. She had been compelled to "lock away" her soul by a yogic act in order to prevent it from following him. Often she must have relived the moment described above, as for instance in May 1958. "When he left and I had to do the Yoga myself, to be able to take his physical place I could have adopted the attitude of the sage, which is what I did, since

---
1. *Words of the Mother*, CWM 15, p. 298.
2. The Mother: *Notes on the Way*, p. 328 (translation revised).

5. Overman

I was in an unparalleled state of calm when he left. As he left his body and entered into mine, he told me: 'You will continue, you will go right to the end of the work.' It was then that I imposed a calm upon this body, the calm of total detachment. And I could have remained like that.

"But in a way, absolute calm implies withdrawal from action, so a choice had to be made between one or the other. I said to myself: 'I am neither exclusively this nor exclusively that.' And actually, to do Sri Aurobindo's work is to realise the Supramental on earth. So I began that work and, as a matter of fact, this was the only thing I asked of my body. I said to it: 'Now you shall set right everything which is out of order and gradually realise this intermediate overmanhood *[surhumanité]* between man and the supramental being, in other words, what I call the overman *[surhomme]*.' *And this is what I have been doing for the last eight years, and even much more during the past two years, since 1956. Now it is the work of each day, each minute.*

"And that's where I am. I have renounced the uncontested authority of a god, I have renounced the unshakable calm of the sage in order to become the overman *[surhomme]*. I have concentrated everything upon that."[3]

This is as good a place as any, now that we have to relate the Mother's work in some detail, to draw attention to the fact of how much her personality and contribution to the Integral Yoga have been – and are – misjudged, underestimated and even neglected. In the primary years of the Ashram, Sri

---

3. *Mother's Agenda I*, 10 May 1958 (emphasis added). The English translation gives here "supermanhood" and "superman" where the Mother in the original French used the words *surhumanité* and *surhomme*. This is a calamitous mistake, made persistently throughout the English translation of the thirteen volumes of *L'Agenda de Mère* as well as of the six volumes of *Entretiens*. The mistake is calamitous because it misleads the English speaking readers of the Mother about the many years of her effort to realise the overman. So consequential has this widespread mistake been that at present hardly any English speaking disciple, follower, devotee or interested reader is aware of the role and the importance of the overman. The misconception, or rather lack of conception, is still more widespread because many translations in other languages are made not from the French original, but from the faulty English translations.

Aurobindo had time and again to put the record straight about her, as is there for anyone to read in his letters. A male Avatar was a known and acceptable phenomenon, but a female Avatar, who had ever heard of that? And a French one, a *mleccha*, to boot! Sri Aurobindo, withdrawn, always looked majestic, guru-like, Shiva-like; the Mother, approachable and for many years moving among the disciples and Ashram students, changed her aspect according to the circumstances and the necessities. Sri Aurobindo had written thick volumes of learned prose, was a poet of renown, and still wrote letter after letter, sometimes several pages long; the Mother played a little on her harmonium, distributed flowers, and mostly communicated her knowledge orally, sometimes in English, more often in French.

But Sri Aurobindo and the Mother had "the same path from the beginning". In 1920, when Mirra Richard and her husband Paul returned from Japan to India, "the Yoga was waiting for the Mother to continue", wrote Sri Aurobindo. It was on the Mother's advice that he and she descended from the supramentalised Mind into the Vital and then, in a most daring yogic move, from the supramentalised Vital into Matter and below, into the Inconscient. They divided the avataric task: Sri Aurobindo in the physical seclusion of his apartment did the general, fundamental Yoga, of which he communicated to the Mother every progress, every gain, every realisation; the Mother took on the task of building up and guiding the Ashram, a world in miniature: she literally did the Yoga of all the accepted disciples, "taking them into her consciousness as in an egg". When Sri Aurobindo called the Second World War "the Mother's War", he must have had good reasons. And, as her body was constitutionally better for the future effort of supramental transformation, she had to stay on and continue the glorious, gruesome job. It is all there to be studied and meditated upon by the interested.

Never has a Yoga of this magnitude, of this importance been so well documented in so many of its phases. Alas, words are but words, and to a new, ignorant eye it all looks so unusual, fantastic, overblown, and confusing – although the principles are logical and rational, the aim the most important and glorious possible, the protagonists human even if in part divine, and their thought practicable for every individual attracted to it. But, you know, what have all those grandiloquent expectations come to? Where is the superman? Where is the new, divine world? Has the world ever been more inhuman and bewildering than now, at the turn of the millennium?

So much is new in this adventure of Sri Aurobindo and the Mother. Here is an Avatar not semi-mythical as in the great epics of the past, but in the flesh, talking, eating, sleeping, writing, riding in a car, being ill, breaking his thigh, having been married and even more than once. And this Avatar is not solely male, as all the others were in the past, but also female; and he/she maintains that they have the same consciousness in their two bodies. Here is an idea that the evolution is to take a gigantic quantum jump now, possibly in our lifetime – not millions of years ago, and not only within the limits of our imagination but contriving something better than paradise! Here is a spiritual practice, called Integral Yoga, demanding the mastery of the whole range of yogas perfected before and recognised as valid, a mastery not to reach liberation, Nirvana, the Absolute or Brahmaloka, but intending the transformation of this whole problematical planet and the founding of heaven here. With the intention of transforming the body, even, of becoming embodied gods on the Earth, of awakening a divine consciousness in the cells! Too fantastic to deign worthwhile considering?

But in whatever way one judges the personalities, the intentions and the work done by Sri Aurobindo and the Mother, no sincere critic can deny the coherence of the vision and the greatness of their effort to turn it into reality. That the world is very little aware of it, is no criterion for evaluation, as it is not a factor in the elaboration of that vision. For they have dug the foundations "to front the years", and in those foundations is built a spiritual Force to assure the *automatic* realisation of the Work they, as the Avatar of the Supermind, had come to perform. As they were one, none of the two was "greater" than the other. And if the above is true, then the difference between both can only arise from our ignorance, from our lack of insight into who they were and what they did.

"This is what I have been doing ..."

Let us, at this point of our enquiry concerning overman, repeat what the Mother said to K.D. Sethna in June 1953 about the Mind of Light: "The Supermind has descended long ago – very long ago – into the mind and even into the vital: it was working in the physical also but indirectly through those intermediaries. The question was about the direct action of the Supermind in the physical. Sri Aurobindo said it could be possible only if the physical mind received the supramental light: the physical mind was the instrument for direct action upon the most material. This physical mind receiving the supramental light Sri Aurobindo called the Mind of Light."[4]

After all we have learned in the previous chapter about "the new humanity" to be endowed with the Mind of Light, this new definition of the Mind of Light comes as a surprise. For as far as we know, in *The Supramental Manifestation upon Earth* Sri Aurobindo never even mentioned the physical mind, surely not in this context. The Mind of Light, he wrote, was "the last in a series of descending planes of consciousness in which the Supermind veils itself by a self-chosen limitation or modification"; it was "a subordinate action of the Supermind", "aware of its affiliation to Supermind", "capable of living in the Truth". Yet, Sethna's report of the Mother's words has to be taken into account not only because it is trustworthy, but also because of what the Mother says in the quotation from 1958 at the beginning of the present chapter. "This [namely, realising the overman, the being to be endowed with the Mind of Light] is what I have been doing for the last eight years, and even more during the past two years ..." This long-term yogic occupation started at the very moment that Sri Aurobindo left his body and

---

4. K.D. Sethna: *The Vision and Work of Sri Aurobindo*, p. 105.

charged her with it. What entered into her body, palpably, was all the supramental Force he had accumulated in his – the Force that was the beginning of the formation of overman.[5]

Secondly, in the Mother's *Entretiens,* her "questions and answers" at the Playground, she sometimes talked on appropriate occasions about her personal yogic experiences and progress. The word that crops up time and again in those brief glimpses of her inner life and work is "cells": their consciousness, aspiration and transformation. Might Sri Aurobindo have expanded on the transformation of the body cells if he had had the time to complete his last series of articles? The lack of reference to the physical cells which, as we shall see, play such an important part in the transformational process, certainly is an argument in favour of the supposition that the series of articles remained unfinished.

Sri Aurobindo has, however, in *The Life Divine* the following words, already quoted before but deserving our renewed attention: "When the powers of any grade descend completely into us, it is not only our thought and knowledge that are affected, – the substance and very grain of our being and consciousness, all its states and activities are touched and penetrated and can be remoulded and wholly transmuted. Each stage of this ascent is therefore a general, if not a total, conversion of the being into a new light and power of a greater existence."[6] Any yogic siddhi has repercussions in the adhara of the yogi, but such effects remain limited to the person having the siddhi. The siddhis the most recent Avatars worked out for humankind – Rama, Krishna, the Buddha, Christ – were to become permanent psychological properties, qualities or possibilities within the human species. As Sri Aurobindo and the Mother had come to initiate a new species, the consequences of their siddhis had to be not only psychological but also physical, material, and this was the reason of their unprecedented difficulty.

---

5. Sri Aurobindo kept his vital and mental supramentalised body-sheaths, consciously descending with them into death and now existing in them in his supraphysical "dwelling", referred to several times by the Mother in the *Agenda.*
6. Sri Aurobindo: *The Life Divine,* p. 938.

Conclusion

Sri Aurobindo had seen that an intermediary species or variety of beings, called by him "the new humanity" and by the Mother "overman" *(le surhomme),* would be necessary to make the appearance of "superman", the supramental being, possible on the Earth, as the gap between Mind and Supermind was too huge for a direct transformation. A new species necessitates a newly evolved, higher physical embodiment, "a greater existence". Sri Aurobindo had started realising such an embodiment in the cells of his body, pulling down the supramental Force into them. When the general cosmic circumstances proved to be such that the supramental transformation leading to the superman was possible only by descending consciously into death, Sri Aurobindo transferred his evolutionary acquisition to the Mother with the instruction to continue the work. This she did at once. Now she was burdened not only with the guidance of the Ashram, she was in charge of the full avataric Yoga too.

On that 5th of December, the Mother suspended all activities in the Ashram for twelve days. The first *Entretien* we have is dated 21 December 1950: exactly twelve days later. There she sat, fully present again, but now alone in this physical universe, with the responsibility on her shoulders of making the impossible possible. The talks she gave at the Playground were actually French classes for the students of the Ashram School; interested adult Ashramites were allowed too. But she talked from the very beginning about all possible topics under the sun. Those talks as a whole form an impressive teaching in their own right. It is true of course that what she said expressed essentially the same vision Sri Aurobindo had given shape in his prose writings and in his poetry, and she commented in many "classes" on texts by Sri Aurobindo, but the *Entretiens* bear distinctly a personal stamp, with roots deep in her own experiences. The audience could ask any question that popped up into their head – and that sometimes she made pop up into their heads.

As early as on 4 January 1950, she talked about "the work of physical transformation, that is the most difficult of all things".[7] On 26 February, less than two months later, she spoke about the "gnostic", i.e. the supramental consciousness, and concluded her talk with the words: "I am telling you that this evening because what has been done, what has been realised by one can be realised by the others. It is enough that one body has been able to realise this, one human body, to have the assurance that it *can* be done. You should consider it still very far into the future, but you may say: 'Yes, the gnostic life is certain, for it has begun to realise itself.'"[8] That "one", the "one body" that had been "able to realise that, one human body", naturally was hers.

Again some six weeks later, on 19 April, the Mother told her Playground audience that what had been up to then a "psychological" Yoga, had now become a "material" Yoga, a Yoga of Matter, of the cells of the body. It is in the cells that we are Matter, they are its presence in us and our direct access to it. Now the consciousness in the cells themselves began to aspire and surrender to the Divine, tried to establish the complete equanimity, which is the precondition of the Integral Yoga, and became aware of the inherent unity of all things. "Now it [the offering of everything to the Divine] has become the very movement of the cellular consciousness. All weaknesses, all responses to adverse suggestions – by this I mean the little things that happen every moment in the cells – are taken up in the same movement of offering. And that comes sometimes in waves, so much so that the body has the impression that it will lose consciousness because of the assault. But then comes a light so warm, so profound, so sweet, so powerful, that puts everything back in order, in its place, and opens the way to the transformation. Such moments are very difficult moments in the life of the body. One feels that there is now only one thing that takes the decisions: the Supreme Will. There is no longer any other support – no support, neither the support that habit

---

7. The Mother: *Questions and Answers 1950-51*, p. 19.
8. Ibid., p. 159. All texts of the Mother have been checked against the original French and corrected where necessary.

gives, nor to the support of the knowledge, nor the support of the will: all the supports have vanished. There is only the Supreme ... Aspiration in the cellular consciousness for perfect sincerity of consecration."[9]

In March 1953, the Mother said: "I tell you: Only if you are sincere in all the elements of your being, up to the very cells of your body, and only if your whole being integrally wants the Divine, are you sure of the victory, but on no less a condition."[10] The invisible work of the transformation of the cells was continuing. She could not tell much about it, not only because many of the students in the Playground were so very young and would not understand, but also because it was a principle with her never to limit or distort an ongoing experience by formulating it into words and thus fixing it.

By the year 1954, however, the transformation of the cells, at this stage of the creation of overman, reached something like a climax. 24 February: "[The conscious, meticulous occupation with the body] is an enormous work. Yet, it is what must be done if one hopes to transform one's body. It must in the first place be put in complete harmony with the inner consciousness. And that requires working in each cell, one might say, in each petty activity, in every activity of the organs."[11]

21 April 1954: "It will take a number of years before we can speak knowledgeably about how this is going to happen [the transformation of the body], all that I can tell you is that it has begun. If you read attentively the next issue of the *Bulletin* ... you will see that it has begun."[12] In the issue referred to, the Mother published *Some Experiences of the Body Consciousness* and *New Experiences of the Body Consciousness*. Without the titles these experiences would read just like other "psychological" yogic experiences. The difference, nevertheless, is enormous. This was no longer a Yoga in which the consciousness located in and above the Mind was instrumental but the consciousness in

---

9. The Mother: *Questions and Answers 1950-51*, p. 339.
10. The Mother: *Questions and Answers 1953*, p. 7.
11. The Mother: *Questions and Answers 1954*, p. 36.
12. Ibid., p. 111.

the cells, of which few people are aware that it exists. Yet if Matter was to be transformed, divinised, it was this consciousness of the cells that had to be transformed and divinised.

Now that, thanks to the discoveries of Science, we are in some way aware of the complexity of a cell (and of an atom, etc.), it seems hardly amazing that some form of consciousness, very different from ours, is at work there, for the simple question is how, otherwise, it all would keep together and working in such a complex way. But in our daily life the physical consciousness of the cells makes itself felt only in the feeling of a vague bodily heaviness and sometimes in a mechanical repetition of some suggestions, physical impressions or elementary remembrances. But if Matter is to become divine, then it is exactly this lowest form of physical consciousness, directly in contact with Matter and supporting it, that has to become divinised. This better than anything else may give an idea of the enormous gap to be bridged and of the necessity of a step in between the human and the supramental being – which is what the Mother was working at.

In the *Experiences of the Body Consciousness*[13] we read: "When we speak of transformation, the word still has for us a vague meaning. It gives us the impression that something is going to happen and all will be well as a consequence. The notion reduces itself almost to this: if we have difficulties, the difficulties will disappear; those who are ill will be cured of their illness; if the body is infirm and incapable, the infirmities and incapacities will be removed; and so on. But as I have said, it is all very vague, it is only an impression. Now a remarkable thing about the body consciousness is that it is unable to know a thing with precision and in full detail except when it is on the point of accomplishing it. So, when the process of transformation becomes clear, when one is able to know through what sequence of movements and changes the total transformation will take

---

13. The body consists of organs and other parts, the organs and other parts consist of cells: the body consists of cells. The body, the organs and the cells, all have a consciousness of their own, but their interconnectedness sometimes causes confusion about the definition of the various forms of consciousness. In this case, the Mother clearly writes about the consciousness of the cells.

place – in what order, in what way, so to speak: which things will come first, which things will follow – when everything will happen in full detail, that will be a sure indication that the hour of realisation is near. Because each time you perceive a detail with exactness, it means that you are ready to accomplish it.

"For the moment, one can have a vision of the whole. For example, it is entirely certain that under the influence of the supramental light, the transformation of the body consciousness will take place first; then will follow a progress in the mastery and control of all the movements and functions of all the organs of the body; afterwards this mastery will change little by little into a sort of radical modification of the movement and then of the constitution of the organs themselves. All that is certain, although the perception of it is not precise enough. But what will finally take place – when the various organs have been replaced by centres of concentration of different forces, qualities and natures, each of which will act according to its own special mode – all this is still merely a conception and the body does not comprehend it very well, because it is still far from realisation and the body can truly comprehend only that which it is on the point of being able to do."[14] Fully involved in the process of transformation, the Mother sketched here the programme of what she would work out in the years to come.

19 May 1954: "It is as though the cells themselves burst into an aspiration, into a call."[15]

3 November 1954: "Each part of the being has it own aspiration, which takes on the nature of the aspiring part. There is even a physical aspiration … The cells of the body understand what the transformation will be, and, with all their strength, with all the consciousness they contain, they aspire for this transformation. The very cells of the body – not the central will, thought or emotion – the cells of the body open in this way to receive the [supramental] Force."[16]

Within four years, the Mother, supported from behind by

---

14. *Words of the Mother*, CWM 15, pp. 300-01.
15. The Mother: *Questions and Answers 1954*, p. 140.
16. Ibid., pp. 391-92.

5. Overman

the work of Sri Aurobindo in the invisible realms, had achieved an enormous amount of work, without anybody knowing. Yes, she had given a hint from time to time, but who had even noticed? Then, towards the end of 1954, the situation seems to have grown critical. On 31 December her traditional message for the new year was distributed: "No human will can finally prevail against the Divine's Will. Let us put ourselves deliberately and exclusively on the side of the Divine, and the Victory is ultimately certain."[17] "This message", she commented, "was written because it is foreseen [by herself] that next year will be a difficult year and there will be many inner struggles and perhaps even outer ones.[18] So I tell all of you what attitude you should take in these circumstances. These difficulties may last not only twelve months – one full year, that is – but fourteen months. And during these fourteen months you must make an effort never to lose the attitude about which I am going to speak to you now"[19] – which was an attitude of utter equanimity, whatever the inner and outer circumstances, and total surrender. This was an astonishing prediction, as we shall see presently.

The difficulties the Mother spoke about were of course intended to harass and if possible to block the work of the Yoga, and were caused by the forces hostile to it. Of the battles she has fought at that time we know nothing, but as the situation seems to have become critical because the Yoga was about to reach its main objective, they must have been fierce. Something decisive seemed to be imminent. "... One has the impression, really, that it has lasted long enough [the ordinary human condition], that one is fed up with it, that it *has to* change", she said in October 1955. "Well, when one has that kind of impression, one takes all – all one is, all one can, all one has – and one jumps into the fray without ever looking back, come what may."[20] – "Mother", asked a child, "you just said that it is very near ...?" – "What,

---
17. Ibid., p. 454.
18. The Cold War was at its peak.
19. The Mother: *Questions and Answers 1954*, p. 453.
20. The Mother: *Questions and Answers 1955*, p. 330.

very near? The event? Yes, otherwise we would not talk about it."

The "event" happened exactly as foreseen: fourteen months after the day it was announced. And decisive it was: on 29 February 1956 the Supermind descended into the earth-consciousness, a "first" in the evolution of the planet. The event Sri Aurobindo and the Mother had been looking forward to and working for from the beginning, the event that was rendered possible by Sri Aurobindo's descent into death and the Mother's working out of the overman consciousness since then, took place on that day – and the world will never be the same again. (It will become a much better place.)

> A long dim preparation is man's life,
> A circle of toil and hope and war and peace ...
> An endless spiral of ascent and fall
> Until at last is reached the giant point
> Through which his Glory shines for whom we were made
> And we break into the infinity of God.[21]

How essential this descent of the supramental Force into the earth-consciousness was and how all along it was the peak realisation, "the giant point", Sri Aurobindo and the Mother had been working towards, is proven by a categorical text of hers, a direct address to the Divine, noted down in her handwriting: "My Lord, what Thou has wanted me to do I have done. The gates of the Supramental have been thrown open and the Supramental Consciousness, Light and Force are flooding the earth.

"But as yet those who are around me are little aware of it – no radical change has taken place in their consciousness and it is only because they trust my word that they do not say that nothing has truly happened. In addition the exterior circumstances are still harder than they were and the difficulties seem to be cropping up more insurmountable than ever.

"Now that the Supramental is there – for of that I am absolutely certain even if I am the only one upon earth to be aware

---

21. Sri Aurobindo: *Savitri,* p. 24.

of it – is it that the mission of this form [her body or adhara] is ended and that another form is to take up the work in its place? I am putting the question to Thee and ask for an answer – a sign by which I shall know for certain that it is still my work and I must continue in spite of all the contradictions, of all the denials. Whatever is the sign I do not care, but it must be *obvious*."[22]
And obvious it must have been, for she has stayed on.

Acceleration

"The movement has much accelerated; the march forward, the stages succeed each other much more rapidly ... Things change quickly",[23] said the Mother on 15 August 1956, Sri Aurobindo's birthday anniversary. The transformative presence of the mighty Supermind made itself felt.

On 13 February 1957, the Mother talked about illness and its relation to the physical body. What came up in these "questions and answers", twice a week at night, was always something happening in her own Yoga or in the inner life of the people around her – for all that was interconnected, it was one and the same process. This is an important observation for any reader of the *Entretiens*: their spiritual range went far beyond the apparently day-to-day topics asked about and commented upon in that Playground not far from the sea. It was after all the place where the Mother was physically present when she performed the cosmic act of opening the gates for the Supramental Consciousness, so that it could pervade the Earth.

"There is no illness, there is no [physical] disorder that is able to resist the discovery of this secret [the power of getting rid of the ego] and the putting of it into practice, not only in the higher parts of the being but also in the cells of the body. If one knows how to teach the cells the splendour that is within them, if one knows how to make them understand the reality that causes them to exist, that gives them being, then they too enter

---
22. *Champaklal's Treasures*, p. 96 (emphasis in the text).
23. The Mother: *Questions and Answers 1956*, p. 263.

the total harmony, and the physical disorder causing the illness vanishes, as do all other disorders of the being.

"But for that you must be neither cowardly nor fearful. When the physical disorder takes hold of you, you must not be afraid. You must not run away from it, you must face it with courage, tranquility, confidence, with the certitude that the illness is *a falsehood* and that if you turn yourself entirely, in full confidence, with a complete tranquility towards the divine Grace, It will establish itself in the cells as It is established in the depths of the being, and the cells themselves will share in the eternal Truth and Joy."[24] Apart from the light this quotation throws on the ever increasing role of the cells in the Yoga, it also is an indication that the Mother, from that time onwards, began being confronted with the health problems which inevitably accompany the physical transformation and which, to the ordinary eye, are common illnesses or "physical disorders".

It certainly was no coincidence that, on 10 April 1957, she began to read to the Playground audience her own French translation of *The Supramental Manifestation upon Earth*. (For Sri Aurobindo and the Mother there was no such thing as a coincidence: in the unity of Brahman all is connected with all.) In the following *Entretiens,* she returns time and again to the capacities of the body and the attitude required for its transformation.

On 29 May 1957 the Mother says: "[One] can open oneself to the supramental Force which is now active on earth and enter a zone of transition where the two influences meet and interpenetrate: where the consciousness is still mental and intellectual in its way of functioning, but sufficiently permeated by the supramental Power and Force to be able to be the instrument of a higher truth." What she refers to here is unmistakably the Mind of Light.

Then she continues, and this sounds like a victory bulletin: *"At present this state can be realised on earth* by those who have prepared themselves to receive the supramental Force that is manifesting. And in this state – in this state of consciousness – the body can benefit from a condition that is much superior to the

---

24. The Mother: *Questions and Answers 1957-58*, p. 42.

condition it was in before. It can be put into direct contact with the essential truth of its being to the extent that, *spontaneously,* at every moment, it knows instinctively or intuitively what is to be done and that it can do it. As I say, *this state can now be realised* by all those who take the trouble of preparing themselves to receive the supramental Force, to assimilate it and to obey it.

"Of course, there is a higher state than this, namely the state Sri Aurobindo speaks of as the ideal to be fulfilled: the divine life in a divine body. But he himself tells us that this will take time, it is an integral transformation that cannot be achieved in a moment. It will even take quite a long time ... However, it is no longer only a possibility, it is no longer even only a promise for a far-off future: it is something that is being executed. Already one can not only foresee but feel the moment when the body will be able to repeat integrally the experience of the most spiritual part of the being, as the inner spirit has already done, and will itself be able to stand in its bodily consciousness before the supreme Reality, turn towards it integrally and say in all sincerity, in a total self-giving of all its cells: 'To be what Thou art, exclusively, perfectly what Thou art, infinitely, eternally – and very simply.'"[25]

A fortnight later, after having read from Sri Aurobindo's second article in which he writes about the effects of fasting, she says (and it is remarkable how her tone grows ever more forceful and affirmative): *"The only thing* that is really effective is the change of consciousness, the inner liberation through an intimate, constant union, absolute, inevitable, with the vibration of the supramental forces. The concern of every second, the will of all the elements of the being, the aspiration of the entire being, also of all the cells of the body, is this union with the supramental forces, the divine forces. And there is no longer any need at all to worry about what the consequences will be. What has to be, in the play of the universal forces and their manifestation, will be, quite naturally, spontaneously, automatically, there is no need to worry about that. The only thing that

---

25. The Mother: *Questions and Answers 1957-58,* pp. 109-110 (first and third emphasis added).

matters is the constant, total, complete contact – constant, yes, constant – with the Force, the Light, the Truth, the Power, and that ineffable joy of the Supramental Consciousness."[26]

The Mother's talk of 10 July 1957 stands out among her many talks (six volumes of *Questions and Answers*). Here she speaks without interruption in an almost hymnal tone about the new world that is born. This is not literature: in her words vibrate the triumphal accomplishment of the essential aim of the Yoga in which she was involved since the beginning of the century, and the joyful confirmation of the birth of a new world. In the first chapters of this book we have tried to make the importance of the coming and the work of the Avatar comprehensible. We have stressed that his/her intervention in the evolution means a decisive, unprecedented turn into a new, practically indescribable mode of being far beyond the one we are accustomed to: into a divine mode. On 29 February 1956, the realisation of this world was assured because the Consciousness that from that day onwards is giving it shape, touched the Earth and did not withdraw. In this talk now the Mother pronounces the confirmation of that event and its effects. The talk is worth being quoted in full, but we have to restrict ourselves to some extracts.

Having read part of the second chapter of *The Supramental Manifestation upon the Earth,* the Mother says: "It is rather difficult to free oneself from the old habits of being in order to be able to conceive freely of a new life, of a new world. And, naturally, the liberation begins on the highest planes of consciousness: it is easier for the mind or the higher intelligence to conceive of new things than for the vital, for instance, to feel the things in a new way. And it is still more difficult for the body to have a purely material conception of what a new world will be. Yet this perception *must precede* the material transformation; first one *must feel* very concretely the strangeness of the old things, their lack of actuality, if I may say so. One must have the feeling, even materially, that they are obsolete, that they belong

---

26. The Mother: *Questions and Answers 1957-58,* pp. 118-19 (emphasis in the text).

to a past that has no longer a reason to exist."[27] The Mother repeats here what she wrote in the passage from *Some Experiences of the Body Cells* quoted above: "A remarkable thing about the body consciousness is that it is unable to know a thing with precision and in full detail except when it is on the point of accomplishing it." Besides, if ever there was a time when one felt "very concretely the strangeness of the old things" and "their lack of relevance", if ever one had "the feeling, even a material impression, that they are outdated, that they belong to a past which no longer has any purpose", it is now.

In the process of the creation of a new world, the elements of the old world and of the new one exist simultaneously. The old world partly continues to survive up to a certain point and mixes with the first elements of the new world. The new world, at the present moment, "is necessarily a *totally* new experience. One would have to go back to the time when there was a transition from the animal to the human creation to find a similar period, and at that time the consciousness was not sufficiently mentalised to be able to observe, to understand, to feel intelligently – the transition must have taken place in a wholly obscure way. Consequently, what I am speaking about is absolutely new, *unique* in the terrestrial creation, it is something that never had a precedent and that really is a perception, or a sensation, or an impression that is quite strange and new. *(After a silence:)* [There is now] a discrepancy [between] something that is overstaying its time and has nothing but quite a subordinate force of existence, and something totally new, but still so young, so imperceptible, almost weak, one might say: it has not yet the power to impose itself, to assert itself, to take the upper hand, to take the place of the other."[28]

Films were a regular feature in the Ashram Playground. On most occasions the Mother watched them together with the students and the adult Ashramites. Thus she had recently been watching a Bengali film, *Rani Rasmani*, about the rich widow who built the Kali temple in Dakshineshwar for Ramakrishna

---

27. The Mother: *Questions and Answers 1957-58*, p. 145 (emphasis in the text).
28. Ibid., pp. 145-46 (emphasis in the text).

Paramhansa. This film, unexpectedly, had become the occasion of a powerful experience. ("For people who believe that some things are important and other things are not, that there are activities which are helpful to the yoga and others which are not, well, this is one more opportunity to prove that they are wrong. I have always noticed that it is the unexpected things that give you the most interesting experiences."[29])

During the film she suddenly had "in a *concrete, material* way the impression that it [i.e. the traditional world dominated by the gods] was another world, a world that had ceased to be real, alive, an outdated world that had lost its reality, its truth, that had been exceeded, surpassed by something that had taken birth [the supramental world] and was only beginning to take shape, but whose *life* was *so intense*, so true, so sublime that all this [the old world of the gods] became false, unreal, worthless. Then I understood truly – for I understood not with the head, not with the intellect, but with the body (you understand what I mean?), I understood in the cells of the body – that a new world *is born* and is beginning to grow ..."[30]

"... I have announced to you all [after the descent of the Supermind] that this new world was born. But it has been so engulfed, as it were, in the old world that so far the difference has not been very perceptible to many people. Still, the action of the new forces has continued very regularly, very persistently, very steadily, and to a certain extent very effectively. And one of the manifestations of this action was my experience – truly so very new – of yesterday evening. And the result of all this I have noticed step by step in almost daily experiences ...

"Firstly, it [the ideal of Sri Aurobindo and the Mother] is more than a 'new concept' of spiritual life and the divine Reality. This concept was expressed by Sri Aurobindo, I have expressed it myself many a time, and it could be formulated more or less as follows: the old spirituality was an escape from life into the divine Reality, leaving the world where it was and as it was; our new vision, on the contrary, is a divinisation of

---
29. The Mother: *Questions and Answers 1957-58*, p. 146.
30. Ibid., p. 147.

life, a transformation of the material world into a divine world. This has been said, repeated, more or less understood; it is indeed the basic idea of what we want to do. But this could be a continuation of the old world as it was with [little more than] an improvement, a widening of it – and so long as it remains only a concept up there, in the realm of thought, it actually is hardly more than that. However, what has happened, what is really new, is that a new world is *born, born, born*. It is not the old one transforming itself, it is a *new* world that is *born*. And we are now right in the middle of the period of transition in which the two are intermingling – in which the old world still persists all-powerful and entirely dominating the ordinary consciousness, but the new one is slipping in, still very modest, unnoticed – unnoticed in so far that outwardly it does not disturb anything very much, for the time being, and that in the consciousness of most people it is even altogether imperceptible. And yet it is working, growing – until it will be strong enough to assert itself visibly ...

"In the supramental creation *there will no longer be any religions*. The whole life will be the expression, the outflowering into forms of the divine Unity manifesting in the world. And there will no longer be what men now call gods. These great divine beings will themselves be able to participate in the new creation; but to do so, they will have to embody in what one could call 'the supramental substance' on earth. And if some of them choose to remain in their world as they are, if they decide not to manifest physically, their relation with the beings of a supramental world on earth will be a relation of friends, of collaborators, of equals, for the highest divine essence will be manifested in the beings of the new supramental world on earth. When the physical substance is supramentalised, to incarnate on earth will no longer be a cause of inferiority, quite the contrary. It will provide a plenitude which cannot be obtained in any other way.

"But all this is in the future. It is a future that has *begun,* but that will take some time to be realised integrally. Meanwhile we are in a very special situation, extremely special, without any precedent ever. We are now witnessing the birth of a new world that is still very young, very weak – not in its essence, but in its outer manifestation – not yet recognised, not even felt, denied by the majority. But it is there. It is there, making an effort to grow, absolutely *sure* of the result. But the road towards it is a completely new road never before traced out: nobody has gone there, nobody has done that! It is a beginning, *a universal beginning*. It is therefore an absolutely unexpected and unpredictable adventure."[31]

Then, she addressed the following unforgettable call – still standing – to all people who are not stuck in their ways and whose soul is alive: "There are people who love adventure. It is to them that I direct this call, and I tell them: 'I invite you to the great adventure.' It is not a question of repeating spiritually what others have done before us, for our adventure begins beyond that. It is a question of a new creation, entirely new, with all the unforeseen events, risks and hazards it entails – *a real adventure* of which the goal is certain victory, but the road to which is unknown and must be traced step by step in the unexplored. [It is] something that has *never* been in this present universe and that will *never* be again in the same way. If this interests you: all right, come aboard. What will happen to you tomorrow, I cannot say. You must leave behind all that has been foreseen, all that has been planned, all that has been built, and set out into the unknown – come what may! And that is that!"[32]

Overman to Make Superman

What does that mean, a transformed, divinised body – a body of which the cells are not only fully conscious in the way we humans understand consciousness, but divinely conscious? It is a perfection "which now we can hardly conceive", wrote Sri

---

31. The Mother: *Questions and Answers 1957-58,* pp. 149-50 (emphases in the text).
32. The Mother: *Questions and Answers 1957-58,* pp. 150-51 (emphases in the text).

Aurobindo. The Mother sometimes tried to give an idea of the capacities of a supramental body to one or other of the Ashram youth. You want to grasp something out of your reach? Just wish to get it and you got it. "Physically, I shall be able to be here and there at the same time. I shall be able to communicate with many people at the same time ... I shall be free of the fetters of ignorance, pain, mortality and unconsciousness. I shall be able to do many things at the same time. The transparent, luminous, strong, light, elastic body won't need any material things to subsist on ... It will be a true being, perfect in proportion, very, very beautiful and strong, light, luminous or else transparent ..."[33]

And the Mother added: "The human body is closer to the animal than to the [supramental] body. It reacts like an animal, subsists like an animal. There is almost no difference between a man and an animal."[34] And there lies the problem: in the enormous difference between our present state and the envisioned, godlike one. "... As the human body had to come into existence with its modification of the previous animal form and its erect figure of a new power of life and its expressive movements and activities serviceable and necessary to the principle of mind and the life of a mental being, so too a body must be developed with new powers, activities or degrees of a divine action expressive of a truth-conscious being and proper to a supramental consciousness and manifesting a conscious spirit", writes Sri Aurobindo.

And he goes on: "While the capacity for taking up and sublimating all the activities of the earth-life capable of being spiritualised must be there, a transcendence of the original animality and the actions incurably tainted by it or at least some saving transformation of them, some spiritualising or psychicising of the consciousness and motives animating them and the shedding of whatever could not be transformed, even a change of what might be called its instrumental structure, its functioning and organisation, a complete and hitherto unprecedented

---
33. Mona Sarkar: *Sweet Mother: Harmonies of Light II*, pp. 18-19 (noted from memory).
34. Ibid., p. 20.

control of these things must be the consequence or incidental to this total change. These things have been already to some extent illustrated in the lives of many who have become possessed of spiritual powers but as something exceptional and occasional, the casual or incomplete manifestation of an acquired capacity rather than the organisation of a new consciousness, a new life and a new nature."[35]

"This destiny of the body has rarely in the past been envisaged or else not for the body here upon earth; such forms would rather be imagined or visioned as the privilege of celestial beings and not possible as the physical residence of a soul still bound to terrestrial nature. The Vaishnavas have spoken of a spiritualised conscious body, *cinmaya deha*; there has been the conception of a radiant or luminous body, which might be the Vedic *jotirmaya deha*. A light has been seen by some radiating from the bodies of highly developed spiritual persons, even extending to the emission of an enveloping aura and there has been recorded an initial phenomenon of this kind in the life of so great a spiritual personality as Ramakrishna. But these things have been either conceptual only or rare and occasional and for the most part the body has not been regarded as possessed of spiritual possibility or capable of transformation ... More ordinarily in the spiritual tradition the body has been regarded as an obstacle, incapable of spiritualisation or transmutation and a heavy weight holding the soul to earthly nature and preventing its ascent either to spiritual fulfilment in the Supreme or to the dissolution of its individual beings in the Supreme ... If a total transformation of the being is our aim, a transformation of the body must be an indispensable part of it; without that no full divine life on earth is possible."[36]

But there remains that huge gap to be bridged between the human and the supramental physicality. As long as bodies are formed by the method of procreation which is the sexual process, they will not be transformable into the refined adharas needed to embody a supramental being. The principal reason

---
35. Sri Aurobindo: *Essays in Philosophy and Yoga,* pp. 538-39.
36. Ibid., pp. 539-40.

5. Overman

is that the sexual process inevitably involves an element of the Inconscient, the basis of gross Matter, and that the Inconscient is irreconcilable with Supermind. "... The necessity of a physical procreation", writes Sri Aurobindo, "could only be avoided if new means of a supraphysical kind were evolved and made available. A development of this kind must necessarily belong to what is now considered as the sphere of the occult and the use of concealed powers of action or creation not known or possessed by the common mind of the race ...

"If there is some reality in the phenomenon of materialisation and dematerialisation claimed to be possible by occultists[37] and evidenced by occurrences many of us have witnessed, a method of this kind would not be out of the range of possibility. For in the theory of the occultists and in the gradation of the ranges and planes of our being which Yoga-knowledge outlines for us there is not only a subtle physical force but a subtle physical Matter intervening between life and gross Matter, and to create this subtle physical substance and precipitate the forms thus made into our grosser materiality is feasible ...

"A soul wishing to enter into a body or form for itself a body and take part in a divine life upon earth might be assisted to do so or even provided with such a form by this method of direct transmutation, without passing through birth by the sex process or undergoing any degradation or any of the heavy limitations in the growth and development of its mind and material body inevitable to our present way of existence. It might then assume at once the structure and greater powers and functionings of the truly divine material body which must one day emerge in a progressive evolution to a totally transformed existence both of life and form in a divinised earth-nature."[38]

All this shows that Sri Aurobindo was fully aware of the

---

37. "Occultism means rightly the use of the higher powers of our nature, soul, mind, life-force and the faculties of the subtle physical consciousness to bring about results on their own or on the material plane by some pressure of their own secret law and its potentialities, for manifestation and results in human or earthly mind and life and body or in objects and events in the world of Matter." (Sri Aurobindo: *Essays in Philosophy and Yoga*, p. 548)
38. Sri Aurobindo: *Essays in Philosophy and Yoga*, pp. 548-49.

problem of the transformation of the animal-human body, and that he suggested a possible solution to it. We now again take up the thread of the Mother's effort to solve precisely this problem. On 4 December 1957 she said: "The problem before us is: *How will this higher form be created?* ... Will it be by a process to be imagined that this [present human] form will little by little transform itself in order to create a new one? Or will it be by some other means, still unknown to us, that the new form [of the supramental being] will appear in the world? What I mean is: will there be a continuity or will there be a sudden appearance of something new? Will there be a progressive transition between what we are now and what our inner spirit aspires to become, or will there be a gap? In other words, shall we be obliged to drop this present human form and wait for the appearance of a new form – an appearance the process of which we do not foresee and which will have no relation with what we are now? May we hope that this body, which is our present means of earthly manifestation, will have the possibility of transforming itself progressively into something that will be able to express a higher life, or will it be necessary to give up this form entirely to enter into another that does not yet exist upon the earth?"[39]

At the time this *Entretien* was due to be published, the Mother added: "Why not both? Both will exist at the same time, the one does not exclude the other. The one will be transformed and be like a rough sketch of the other." This reminds us of Sri Aurobindo's "a first sketch of supermanhood". "And the other, perfect, will appear when the first one will be existing. For both have their beauty and their reason of existence, therefore they will both be there. The mind always tries to make choices, decisions, but things do not work like that. Even all that we can imagine is much less than what will be. In truth, anyone who has an intense aspiration and an inner certitude will be called upon to realise it ... Just as all sorts of possible intermediaries have been found between the animals and man, possible intermediaries that have not remained, so [now too] there will be all

---
39. The Mother: *Questions and Answers 1957-58*, p. 233.

sorts of possible intermediaries: each individual will try in his own way, and all this together will help in preparing the future realisation."[40]

A few months earlier she had already said: "There are two things. There is the possibility of a purely supramental creation on the one hand, and [on the other hand] the possibility of a progressive transformation of a physical body into a supramental body, or rather of a human body into an overman body *[surhumain]*. In the latter case, it would be a progressive transformation which could take a certain number of years, probably a fairly considerable number, and which would produce a being that would no longer be a human being related to the animal, but that would neither be the supramental being formed fully free of any kind of animality, for the present origin [of man] is necessarily an animal origin. This means that a transmutation may take place, a transformation sufficient to liberate [the new being] from its [animal] origin, yet [that new being] would not be a supramental creation pure and simple. Sri Aurobindo said that there would be an intermediary race – a race or some individuals maybe, one does not know – an intermediary degree that would serve as a transition or that would become permanent according to the requisites and the necessities of the creation. But if one starts from a body generated in the way human bodies are at present, the result will never be the same as a being generated entirely according to the supramental method and process. It will perhaps be more of the kind of the overman *[surhumain]* in the sense that every animal likeness may disappear, but it will not be able to have the absolute perfection of a body that is purely supramental in its generation."[41]

On 25 September 1957, the Mother read a passage from Chapter 6 of *The Supramental Manifestation upon Earth;* the last paragraph of this chapter goes as follows: "At its highest it [i.e. the new humanity] would be capable of passing into the Supermind and from the new race would be recruited the race of supramental beings who would appear as the leaders

---
40. Ibid., p. 234.
41. Ibid., pp. 130-31.

of the evolution in earth-nature." Her comment, now wholly understandable and of obvious importance: "This was certainly what he expected of us, what he conceived of as the overman *[surhomme]*, who must be the intermediate being between humanity as it is and the supramental being created in the supramental way, in other words: in no way part of the animal life any longer and freed from all animal needs.

"As we are, we have been procreated in the ordinary way, the animal way, and as a consequence something of this animal origin will remain, even if we transform ourselves. The supramental being as he [Sri Aurobindo] conceived it, is *not at all* formed in the ordinary animal way, but directly, through a process that for the time being still seems occult to us, but that is a direct manipulation of forces and substance in such a way that the body is a 'materialisation' and not a formation according to the ordinary animal principle.

"It is quite obvious that intermediary beings are necessary, and that it is these intermediary beings who must find the means to create beings of the Supermind. And there is no doubt that, when Sri Aurobindo wrote this, he was convinced that this is what we have to do.

"I think I *know* – that it is now certain that we shall realise what he expects of us. It is no longer a hope, it is a certainty. Only, the time needed for this realisation will be long or short according to our individual effort, our concentration, our goodwill, and the *importance* we give to this fact. To the inattentive observer things may seem to be very much what they were in the past, but to somebody who knows how to look and is not deceived by appearances things are going well. Let each one do his best and it may be that not many years will have to go by before the first visible results become apparent to all.

"It is for you to know whether this interests you more than anything else in the world. There is a moment when the body itself finds that there is *nothing in the world* so much worth living for as this, the transformation; that there is nothing which can be of an interest comparable with this passionate interest for the transformation. It is as though all the cells of the body were thirsting for that Light that wants to manifest. They cry out for it, they find an intense joy in it, and they are *sure* of the Victory.

"This is the aspiration that I am trying to share with you, and you will understand that everything else in life is dull, insipid, futile, worthless in comparison with that: the transformation in the Light."[42]

The Supramental Ship

The Mother knew from experience that the supramental world was already existing, that it was there, waiting to dock with the world we are living in, "a world that wants to incarnate in the world".[43] Sri Aurobindo has often explained that within the Supermind itself there exist uncountable layers or worlds, hierarchically, each more concrete than our gross material world and with its own splendid beings – the "brilliances" – all greater than the gods. We may suppose that the supramental world ready to contact the material one was the nearest and therefore the lowest in that hierarchy, but supramental it was nonetheless. The problem therefore now consisted in the connection of that supramental world with the material world, for the kind and density of both substances is so different.[44] To put it metaphorically: the one is sun-stuff, the other is mud. (This will be a continuous point of concern for the Mother's body

---

42. The Mother: *Questions and Answers 1957-58*, pp. 190-91.
43. The Mother: *Notes on the Way*, p. 317.
44. If human beings came in the presence of the Supermind "each of them would disappear", said the Mother. The reason is that the Supermind is an absolute Truth-Consciousness whose substance of supramental Light would cause the falsehood, present to a high degree in *all* human beings, to disappear in the blink of an eye. "When That comes, when the Lord is there, there is not one person in a thousand who is not terrified. And not in their mind, not in their thought: in their substance [in the cells of their body]. Suppose then, just suppose that it happens, that a certain being [she herself, for instance] becomes the condensation and expression, a formula of the supreme Power, of the supreme Light: just imagine what would happen then!" (The Mother: *Notes on the Way*, p. 51).

in the coming years: the dosing of the transforming power, in order to prevent her material body from disintegrating.)

The Mother knew perfectly well what the supramental world was like; she had been there often and, as we will see, she even had a permanent presence or emanation there (as in any other world). On 5 February 1958, she gave a simile to make the children understand how the Divine works out his manifestation within the eternal plenitude of the Reality. "All is absolutely determined, for all *is* from all eternity, and yet the path traversed [by the Consciousness] has a freedom and unpredictability that is also absolute." The movement of the Consciousness within itself she called "the great Journey". "This is how there can exist simultaneously worlds that have no apparent relationship with each other, but that nevertheless coexist and are discovered gradually, which every time gives the impression of a new creation.

"Seeing things in this way, one can understand that simultaneously with this physical world as we know it, with all its imperfections, all its limitations, all its ignorance, there are one or several other worlds which exist in their own regions, and they are of such a different nature from ours here that to us they are practically non-existent, for we have no contact with them. But when the eternal great Journey moves from one world to another, by the very fact of this movement of the eternal Consciousness the link will necessarily be created, and the two worlds will gradually enter into contact with each other.

"Truly, this is what is actually happening now, and we can say with certitude that the supramental world already exists, but that the time has come for it to become the goal of the Journey of the supreme Consciousness, that little by little a conscious link will be formed between our world and that new one, and that they will have a new relation as a result of this new turn of the journey." And the Mother added: "This explanation is as good as any other, and it is perhaps easier to understand for people who are not metaphysicians. As to me, I like it!"[45]

When she said this, she had just had a mighty experience,

---

45. The Mother: *Questions and Answers 1957-58*, p. 266.

on the 3rd of February, of which these reflexions were the result. Experiences she had by the dozen, not to say by thousands, for her whole life was *one* uninterrupted flow of experiences. Only, it so happened from time to time that an external or internal occasion, in herself or in "the family of the aspiration" she was guiding, caused her to reveal something to others. Compared to the whole of the experiences of Sri Aurobindo and the Mother's Yoga, we know just about nothing – the incredible literature they have left us, the richest spiritual literature in history, is but crumbs of what they knew and have gone through. These crumbs, however, allow us like adventurous Tom Thumbs to retrace to a certain extent the path they have hewn in "the virgin forest", and they contain the magic power, when assimilated, to trigger any experience needful for the personal progress on that path. The experience the Mother had on 3 February 1958 is a revealing one, but once again we have to summarise.

She starts by comparing the world of the animals with the one of the humans: "Between the beings of the supramental world and the humans almost the same separation exists as between humans and animals." She had a long and thorough experience with animals, especially with cats.[46] "They do not understand, they do not *see* us as we are and they suffer because of us. We are a constant enigma to them. Only a very tiny part of their consciousness has a link with us. And it is the same thing for us when we try to look at the supramental world. Only when the link of consciousness is established shall we see it – and even then only the part of our being which has undergone transformation in this way will be able to see it as it is – otherwise the two worlds would remain apart like the animal and the human worlds.

"The experience I had on the 3rd of February is proof of this. Before that I had an individual subjective contact with the supramental world, whereas on the 3rd of February I moved in it concretely, as concretely as I once used to walk in Paris, in a world *that exists in itself,* outside all subjectivity ... Here is the experience as I dictated it immediately afterwards."

---
46. See Chapter 8 in Georges Van Vrekhem's *The Mother: The Story of Her Life.*

The Mother reads[47]: "The supramental world exists permanently and I am there permanently in a supramental body. I had the proof of this even today when my earth-consciousness went there and remained there consciously between two and three o'clock in the afternoon. Now I know that what is lacking for the two worlds to unite in a constant and conscious relation is an intermediate zone between the physical world as it is and the supramental world as it is. This zone remains to be built, both in the individual consciousness and the objective world, and it is being built. When I used to speak of the new world which is being created, it was of this intermediary zone that I was speaking. And similarly, when I am on this side, that is, in the field of the physical consciousness, and I see the supramental power, the supramental light and substance constantly penetrating matter, it is the construction of this zone which I see and in which I participate.

"I was on a huge ship, which was a symbolic representation of the place where the work is going on. This ship, as large as a city, is fully organised, and it had certainly already been functioning for some time, for its organisation was complete. It is the place where the people are trained who are destined for the supramental life. These people, or at least part of their being, had already undergone a supramental transformation, for the ship itself and everything on board was neither material, subtle-physical, vital or mental: [everything consisted of] a supramental substance. This substance was of the most material supramental, the supramental substance nearest to the physical world, the first to manifest. The light was a mixture of gold and red, forming a uniform substance of a luminous orange. Everything was like that. The light was like that, the people were like that – everything had that colour, although in various shades, which made it possible to distinguish things from each other. The general impression was of a world without shadows. The atmosphere was full of joy, calm, order. Everything went in an orderly way and in silence. And at the same time one could

---

47. The Mother: *Questions and Answers 1957-58*, p. 271 ff.

see all the details of an education, of a training in all fields, through which the people on board were being prepared.

"This immense ship had just reached the shore of the supramental world and a first group of people who were destined to become the future inhabitants of the supramental world were to go ashore ... I was in charge of the whole enterprise from the beginning and throughout the proceedings. I had prepared all the groups myself. I stood on the ship at the head of the gangway, calling the groups one by one and sending them ashore ...

"On the ship the nature of the objects was not as we know it on earth. For instance, the clothes were not made of fabric, and what looked like fabric was not manufactured: it formed part of the body, it was made of the same substance [as the body] which took different forms. It had a kind of plasticity. When a change had to be made, it took place not by any artificial and external means but by an inner movement, a movement of the consciousness, which gave that substance its shape and appearance. Life created its own forms. There was *one single substance* in everything; it changed the quality of its vibration according to need and usage."

Then the Mother describes herself as she was on that ship: "My upper part, particularly the head, was not much more than a silhouette of which the contents were white with an orange fringe. The more down towards the feet, the more the colour looked like that of the people on the ship, that is to say orange; the more upwards, the more it was translucent and white, with less red. The head was only a contour with a brilliant sun in it. Rays of light radiated from it, which were actions of the will.

"As for the people I saw on board the ship, I recognised them all. Some were from here, from the Ashram, others were from elsewhere, but I know them too. I saw everybody, but as I knew that I would not remember them all when coming back, I decided not to mention any names ...

"When I came back I knew, simultaneously with the recollection of the experience, that the supramental world is permanent, that my presence there is permanent, and that only a missing link was needed for enabling the connection in the consciousness and in the substance, and it is this link which is now being established ..."

When the Mother had finished reading the report of her experience, she commented upon it. "One thing – and I want to tell you this – seems to me at the moment to be the most essential difference between our world and the supramental world (and it is only after having gone there consciously, with the consciousness that normally is active here, that this difference has become apparent to me in what one might call its enormity): everything here, except what goes on within, very deep within, appeared to me absolutely artificial. None of the values of the ordinary life, of the physical life, are based on the truth ... This artificiality, this insincerity, this complete lack of truth became so shockingly apparent to me that one wonders how, in so false a world, we can make any valid evaluations.

"But instead of becoming despondent, morose, rebellious, or dissatisfied, one rather has the feeling of what I was telling you at the end [of the text she read]: of something so madly ridiculous that for days I was seized with uncontrollable laughter when I looked at things and at people – an uncontrollable laughter, totally inexplicable except to myself, because of the ridicule of the situations." Those who are turning the Yoga of Sri Aurobindo and the Mother into a religion or a sect, in spite of their warnings, better keep this in mind.[48]

And the Mother finished with the words: "When I invited you on a journey into the unknown, a journey of adventure, I did not know I was so close to the truth. And I can promise those who are ready to attempt the adventure that they will make very interesting discoveries."[49]

---

48. Time and again Sri Aurobindo and the Mother have warned against the danger of making their vision into a new religion. "... *No new religion, no dogmas, no fixed teachings.* One must avoid – one must avoid at all costs – that this should become a new religion." (The Mother: *Notes on the Way*, p. 133)
49. The Mother: *Questions and Answers 1957-58*, pp. 277-78.

5. Overman

With Lightning Speed

On 16 April 1958, the last paragraph of the passage the Mother read from *The Life Divine* went as follows: "If, then, man is incapable of exceeding mentality, he must be surpassed and Supermind and superman must manifest and take the lead of the creation. But if his mind is capable of opening to what exceeds it, then there is no reason why man himself should not arrive at Supermind and supermanhood or at least lend his mentality, life and body to an evolution of that greater term of the Spirit manifesting in Nature."[50] The last sentence is one of the several pointers in *The Life Divine* to the possibility, if not the necessity, of an intermediary being between the human and the supramental species. The Mother's comment is not only important, it is also a kind of summary of everything we have examined up to here. She is speaking, throughout, of the overman.

"Anyway, we have now arrived at a certitude, since there is already a beginning of realisation. We have the proof that in certain conditions the ordinary state of humanity can be exceeded and a new state of consciousness worked out which enables at the very least a conscious relation between mental and supramental man.

"It can be affirmed with certainty that there will be an intermediate specimen between the mental and the supramental being, a kind of overman [surhomme] *who will still have the qualities and in part the nature of man, which means that he will still belong in his most external form to the human being [i.e. species] of animal origin, but that he will transform his consciousness sufficiently to belong, in his realisation and activity, to a new race, a race of overmen* [surhommes].[51]

"This species may be considered a transitional species, for it is to be foreseen *that it will discover the means of producing new beings without going through the old animal method, and it is these beings – who will have a truly spiritual birth – who will constitute the elements of the new race, the supramental race. So we could call*

---

50. Sri Aurobindo: *The Life Divine*, p. 847.
51. In both cases in this paragraph (as elsewhere), *surhomme* has been translated by "superman", which proves how deeply the confusion was and is ingrained.

overmen [surhommes] *those who, because of their origin, still belong to the old method of generation but who, because of their accomplishment, are in conscious and active contact with the new world of supramental realisation.*

"It seems – it is even certain – that the very substance that will constitute this intermediate world, which is already being built, is richer, more powerful, more luminous, more durable, with certain new, subtler, more penetrating qualities, and a kind of innate capacity of universality. It is as if its degree of subtlety and refinement allowed the perception of vibrations in a much more extensive, if not altogether total way, and it abolishes the sensation of division one has with the old substance, the ordinary mental substance." The Mother is here describing the new, more refined kind of Matter necessary for the embodiment of the new species.

In the coming years her descriptions of this new kind of Matter will become more and more detailed, but as early as in *New Experiences of the Body Consciousness* (1954) she had written: "In this intensity the aspiration grows formidable, and in answer to it Thy Presence becomes evident in the cells themselves, giving to the body the appearance of a multicoloured kaleidoscope in which innumerable luminous particles in constant motion are sovereignly reorganised by an invisible and all-powerful Hand."[52]

Essential to the understanding of the Mother's Yoga during the rest of her life is also that her body gradually became more universalised as a consequence of the transformation of its cells. Her (and Sri Aurobindo's) mind and vital had already been universalised, because supramentalised, in the Twenties. The problem of the transformation of the body consisted precisely in the fact that up to now its universalisation had proved impossible and, consequently, that its supramentalisation or divinisation too was impossible, for there is no divinity without universality. We have step by step gained a notion of the fantastic – but on the surface rather logical – transformation that was going on in the Mother.

---

52. *Words of the Mother*, CWM 15, pp. 302-03.

5. Overman

The *Entretien* continues: "There is a subtlety of vibration which renders global, universal perception spontaneous and natural. The sense of division, of separation, vanishes quite naturally and spontaneously with [the presence of] this substance. And this substance is at present almost universally spread out in the atmosphere of the earth ...

"One may conclude from this that the moment one body, of course formed according to the old animal method, is capable of living this consciousness naturally and spontaneously, without any effort, without going out of itself, it proves that it is not an exceptional, unique case, but that it simply is the forerunner of a realisation which, even if it is not general, *can at least be shared by a certain number of individuals* who, moreover, as soon as they share [that realisation], will lose the feeling of being separate individuals and become a living collectivity.

"*This new realisation is proceeding with what one might call lightning speed,* for if we consider time in the usual way, only two years have passed – a little more than two years – from the moment the supramental substance penetrated into the earth-atmosphere [on 29 February 1956] till the moment that this change in the quality of the earth-atmosphere took place [i.e. now]."[53]

---

53. The Mother: *Questions and Answers 1957-58,* pp. 313 ff. (emphasis added).

6.
The Consciousness of the Overman

> *The transition from man to supramental being is accomplished through the overman. There may be a few overmen – there are – who will actually make that transition.*[1]
>
> – the Mother

> *The transitional beings are always in an unstable equilibrium.*[2]
>
> – the Mother

We have now returned to the point where we started in the previous chapter: May 1958, when the Mother reminisced about the moment Sri Aurobindo left his body and transferred to her all the supramental power gathered in it. This was when she said to her already badly battered body (for the Integral Yoga "is not a joke"): "'Now you shall set right everything that is out of order and gradually realise this intermediate overmanhood between man and the supramental being – in other words: what I call the overman.' And this is what I have been doing for the last eight years, and even much more during the past two years, since 1956. Now it is the work of each day, each minute."

Towards the end of November 1959 and at the beginning of December, the Mother had to go through a severe, life-threatening ordeal, the first of many in the coming years. On 26 November she gave her last *Entretien* at the Playground; on 7 December she played her last game of tennis (at the age of 81); on 9 December she stopped leaving the Ashram compound, except on special occasions. What was happening? Now that

---
1. *Mother's Agenda,* 15 April 1972.
2. The Mother: *Notes on the Way*, p. 28.

6. The Consciousness of the Overman

the overman was realised, the Mother took up the supramentalisation of the body; she started building the first supramental body, the archetype of the future supramental species, within her gross material body.

The Mother had realised the possibility for overman, the transitional being, to exist physically on the earth: she had, as it were, created by the partial transformation of her own *adhara* the mould for the overman to appear as an intermediary degree in the evolution of the human and the supramental being. Remember what she said in 1958: "One may conclude from this that the moment one body [i.e. her own], of course formed according to the old animal method, is capable of living this consciousness naturally and spontaneously, without any effort, without going out of itself, it proves that it is not an exceptional, unique case, but that it simply is the forerunner of a realisation which, even if it is not general, *can at least be shared by a certain number of individuals.*"

This having been accomplished, the Mother began another great phase in her yoga: the realisation, through the transformation of her own physicality, of the archetype of the supramental being. These two realisations, far beyond the horizon of our imagination, were the reason why she stayed on in 1956. They were the reason why Sri Aurobindo decided to descend into death as, according to his own words, the Mother's body was better suited than his to undergo this transformation. The Mother even said that, knowing the severity of what was awaiting her in her new incarnation, she had chosen both her parents especially with this factor in view: the robustness of their bodies. The double Avatar had come to establish the Supermind in the consciousness of the earth. It may be guessed that, through their love for humanity, they have shortened the appearance of the supramental being by hundreds, if not thousands, of years.

The Mysteries of the Body

The Mother withdrew, but only in certain ways. She remained bodily in her small apartment on the second floor of the central Ashram building in the Rue de la Marine, and the work increased gradually to the extent that she hardly had any time for herself. For she went on running the Ashram down to the smallest detail, and she received people who wanted to see her for all possible reasons, on an average forty to fifty a day, but at times up to two hundred. And there was also the inner Work of the Yoga, and there was the inner, invisible crowd that came to her with good intentions as well as bad. "I lead a much more busy life than the life I lead downstairs."[3]

The phase of the Yoga which involved the transformation of the body was not something totally new. It was the continuation of the transformation we have been following in the previous chapter, but much more radical. From now onwards it was literally the body cells in ever greater numbers – there are fifty trillion of them – that were doing the Yoga. For a number of those cells were now transformed. Can one imagine what this means: cells of the body, tiny living organisms, that have acquired a spiritual consciousness? The Mother must have read the incomprehension in the mind of the persons she was talking to, for she said so often something like: "It is the experience *of the body*, you understand, physically, materially: the experience of the body!"[4] The aspiration, the equanimity, the sincerity – all basics of the Integral Yoga – were now to become qualities of the cells, practised by the cells, acquired by the cells. But above all there was the surrender, "the Alpha and Omega of the Integral Yoga" (Sri Aurobindo). Surrender was the main occupation of the Mother, day and night. Every cell, every part of the cell had to open to the Light in order to become accessible to it. They had to overcome all the subconscious and

---
3. The Mother: *Notes on the Way*, p. 22. The *Notes on the Way* are extracts from *Mother's Agenda* published from October 1964 onwards in the *Bulletin of Physical Education* of the Sri Aurobindo Ashram. In this chapter we will quote mostly from this book.
4. The Mother: *Notes on the Way*, p. 151.

6. The Consciousness of the Overman

inconscient obscurity and darkness we carry in us, which in fact is the substance we are made of. And there is the memory of the ages, of the previous stages of evolution, that is still present in the cells, for they were there from the beginning.

> Inflicting still its habit on the cells
> The phantom of a dark and evil start
> Ghostlike pursues all that we dream and do.[5]

All that had to be pervaded by the transforming Light, according to the Will of the Supreme. "*Ce que Tu veux*", said the Mother, the palms of both her hands turned upwards in a gesture of complete submission: "What You will". "It is day and night, without interruption: 'What You will, Lord, what You will ...' " – "The only solution, at every moment and in all cases, is *(gesture of self-giving)*. 'What you will', that is to say, the abolition of preference and desire, even the preference of not suffering." – "What I told you is the truth, it is the *only* remedy: to exist only for the Divine; to exist only through the Divine; to exist only in the service of the Divine; to exist only by becoming the Divine."[6] To create the possibility of a higher species taking a body on earth, not only gross Matter had to be refined, but the functioning of the body also had to be refined. Actually, the latter would be a consequence of the former. The functioning of the cells had to be refined, as well as the functioning of the organs. This too Sri Aurobindo foresaw in *The Supramental Manifestation:* "There would have to be a change in the operative processes of the material organs themselves and, it may well be, in their very constitution and their importance; they could not be allowed to impose their limitations imperatively on the new physical life. To begin with, they might become more clearly outer ends of the channels of communication and action, more serviceable for the psychological purposes of the inhabitant, less blindly material in their responses, more conscious of the act and aim of the inner movements and powers which use them and which they are wrongly supposed by the material

---
5. Sri Aurobindo: *Savitri,* p. 140.
6. The Mother: *Notes on the Way,* pp. 171, 222, 259.

man in us to generate and to use. The brain would be a channel of communication of the form of the thoughts and a battery of their insistence on the body and the outside world where they could then become effective directly ... The heart would equally be a direct communicant and medium of interchange for the feelings and emotions ... The will might control the organs that deal with food, safeguard automatically the health, eliminate greed and desire, substitute subtler processes or draw in strength and substance from the universal life-force ...

"It might well be that the evolutionary urge would proceed to a change of the organs themselves in their material working and use and diminish greatly the need of their instrumentation and even of their existence. The centres in the material body ... of which one would become conscious and aware of all goings on in it, would pour their energies into material nerve and plexus and tissue and radiate them through the whole material body; all the physical life and its necessary activities in this new existence could be maintained and operated by these higher agencies in a freer and ampler way and by a less burdensome and restricting method. This might go so far that these organs might cease to be indispensable and even be felt as too obstructive: the central force might use them less and less and finally throw aside their use altogether. If that happened they might waste by atrophy, be reduced to an insignificant minimum or even disappear. The central force might substitute for them subtle organs of a very different character or, if anything material was needed, instruments that would be forms of dynamism or plastic transmitters rather than what we know as organs."[7]

The language is dense and abstract, but the implications are enormous. A complete change of the body and its organs far beyond our imagination is of course necessary to constitute a supramental, divine being. "If a total transformation of the being is our aim, a transformation of the body must be an indispensable part of it; without that no full divine life on earth is possible."[8] Otherwise how would one be able "to be here and

---

7. Sri Aurobindo: *Essays in Philosophy and Yoga*, p. 553 ff.
8. Ibid., p. 540.

6. The Consciousness of the Overman

there at the same time"? How would one be able "to communicate with many people at the same time"? In other words, how would one be able to be godlike in a physical body? Already in the very beginning of *The Life Divine* Sri Aurobindo, taking the example of "wireless telegraphy", predicted that "the physical means for the intermediate transmission of the physical force" must eventually disappear. "For when the laws and forces of the supraphysical are studied with the right starting-point, the means will infallibly be found for Mind directly to seize on the physical energy and speed it accurately upon its errand. There, once we bring ourselves to recognise it, lie the gates that open upon the enormous vistas of the future."[9]

Here now the Mother was studying the laws and forces of the supraphysical with the right starting-point in what she called "microscopic studies". What was going on in her, however, was enormous, fantastic, flabbergasting. The creation of a new, refined form of Matter in Matter?[10] The change of the material organs into their supramaterial essence while alive? How can a heart be changed while it has to go on beating? And yet, this kind of thing was happening in her!

"All habits are undone", she said. "And it is like that with all the functions [of the body]: with the blood circulation, with the digestion, with the respiration – with all the functions. And at the moment of change [from the normal way of functioning into the new one], it is not so that the one suddenly replaces the other: there is a fluid state in between, and that is difficult. It is only this great Faith, wholly immobile, luminous, constant, immutable – the faith in the real existence of the supreme Lord, in the *sole* real existence of the Supreme – that enables everything to continue being apparently the same."[11] If ever there was a great adventure, then this metamorphosis

---

9. Sri Aurobindo: *The Life Divine*, pp. 15-16.
10. "The necessary forms and instrumentations of Matter must remain since it is in a world of Matter that the divine life has to manifest, but their materiality must be refined, uplifted, ennobled, illumined, since Matter and the world of Matter have increasingly to manifest the indwelling spirit." Sri Aurobindo: *Essays in Philosophy and Yoga*, p. 556.
11. The Mother: *Notes on the Way*, pp. 58-59.

was surely it. It was "a battle against a habit that is thousands of years old", a "catastrophic habit". Her entire body was "emptied of its habits and its forces, and then slowly, slowly the cells woke up to their new receptivity and opened to the Divine Influence directly."[12] "The necessities" were bit by bit losing their authority. "All the laws, those laws that were the laws of Nature, have lost what one could call their despotism: it is no longer as it was",[13] the Mother said in 1967. Yet, she was still far from the complete realisation.

Every part of her body was undergoing or had to undergo "a change of master", as she put it: a change "from the ordinary automatic functioning to a conscious functioning under the direct guidance and the direct influence of the Supreme."[14] The whole material body had to be permeated by the Divine. This was, of course, the supreme *siddhi*, and if it is true that every siddhi has an influence, a repercussion on the physical body, then the supreme siddhi must have a supreme, absolute influence. The Mother's day-to-day experiences were baffling and could not have been possible without her avataric Yoga and, yes, the solidity of her physical constitution.

In our experience our body feels like the centre or axis of the material universe, and this feeling is firmly grounded in our ego-sense. Mentally and vitally the Mother had not had an ego for a very long time. But the body, in order to function normally, had naturally continued having its ego-sense. This ego-sense was now being dissolved and replaced by the presence of "the Supreme". How does it feel being in a body when this body is no longer the centre of the material universe? "In the last few days, yesterday and the day before, there was this experience: a kind of consciousness completely decentralised – I am *always* speaking of the physical consciousness, not at all of the higher levels of consciousness – a decentralised consciousness that was

---

12. Ibid., p. 94.
13. Ibid., p. 107.
14. Ibid., p. 33. The Mother did not like to use the word "God", for she found that word "hollow, but dangerously hollow" (p. 78). What is the Divine? "A smiling and luminous immensity" (p. 77), "the splendour of the Presence" (p. 117).

6. The Consciousness of the Overman

here, there, in this body and in that other one. In what people call 'this person' and 'that person', but the notion [of a 'person'] does not exist very much any more."[15] This line of her Yoga, like all others, will develop further and her body will become the body of the earth.

We have seen (cf. 'The Ship from the Supramental World') that the supramental world was there, ready to permeate the gross material world and take its place. The more the Mother's cells became supramentalised, the more she belonged physically to the supramental world too, which means that for years she belonged physically to two worlds, the gross material and the supramental! How does one do that? How does one live in two worlds at the same time, physically – two worlds that are ... worlds apart? This was a serious problem which, at first, she was not able to solve. The transitions from the one world to the other occurred unpredictably and abruptly, with the result that the Mother would faint at the most unexpected moments and in the most inconvenient places. This line too will gradually develop and she will acquire mastery over these kind of transitions.

However, to those surrounding her the faintings and the other tokens of the ongoing transformation looked like symptoms of illnesses. The disciples had no idea what was going on. The first reports, culled from personal conversations, would be published in the *Bulletin* only from October 1964 onwards, and even then the information provided was so sparse and so totally out of the ordinary that nobody gained any better insight into what was happening, not even the most "advanced" disciples. (And who has understood it even now? For a real understanding, a real knowledge is only possible when one is able to repeat the experience. This is at least as important to yoga, a matter of Truth, as it is to Science.)

As a consequence the Mother, from the time of her withdrawal in 1959, was thought to be almost continuously ill. It certainly looked like it. "You are surrounded by people who treat you as

---

15. The Mother: *Notes on the Way*, p. 4.

an ill person, and you know that you are not ill."[16] She stressed vigorously, and in part to counteract the suggestions projected upon her from all sides, that she was never ill: "These are not illnesses, these are functional disorders",[17] she said, caused by the process of transformation. And: "I have nothing to do with an illness from which one gets cured. I cannot get cured! This is the work of transformation!"[18]

All the same, the Mother was constantly in a state of "unstable equilibrium", with one organ after the other, and sometimes several at the same time, being transformed, which meant a temporary suspension of its function and afterwards a completely new, unknown way of functioning ... Who could stand that? And all these changes, suspensions and transformations of course caused a considerable upheaval in the physical body – an upheaval making itself felt by pain. On the one hand there was the glory of the transformation, on the other the terror of it – heaven and hell alternating, sometimes in one and the same moment. "Three minutes of splendour for twelve hours of misery." – "Some seconds of paradise for hours of hell." – "The marvellous moment lasts for a few minutes and is followed by hours of agony." All these are her words.

She went through these ordeals while carrying out her daily routine, from the age of eighty to ninety-five – a routine that would prove too much for most young and healthy people. At that time the Ashram had some thirteen hundred inmates and six hundred students, living and working in numerous buildings. The secretaries and heads of the Ashram departments came for her advice, decisions, signatures and answers to the daily correspondence. The Ashramites met her at least once a year, on their birthday, which was considered by the Mother to be a special day; but many sought to meet her more often when they were in inner or outer difficulty. The children came on their birthday too, and the school was a kind of abiding challenge because the teachers struggled to find ways of applying

---

16. *Mother's Agenda XI*, 16.5.1970.
17. *Mother's Agenda II*, 25.2.1961.
18. *Mother's Agenda III*, 12.6.1962.

the Yoga in the education. In addition there were the visitors of every standing and class, presidents, prime ministers, cabinet ministers of the Indian Union and of the States, kings, princes, gurus, religious leaders, professors, ambassadors, foreigners from all over the world, film actors and other celebrities. And this was only the human crowd.

What Was to be Done, is Done

At the beginning of April 1962, the situation became so critical that some thought the Mother had passed away. As in 1958 and during the following grave ordeals, she was attacked by black magic. Who were the attackers? Powerful beings from the invisible worlds who used human instruments. One of those hostile beings was a "titan" who had been a threat to her life since her birth and who, according to her own report, had actually been born at the same time. Another was the Lord of Falsehood who calls himself the Lord of the Nations; he had assured her that he would cause all possible havoc until she had destroyed him. The "Lord of the Nations" has been the origin of the great wars and all evil in the past century; he was the being by whom Hitler was possessed.[19]

Who were the human instruments? We do not know and it is risky to guess. It is much easier to become the medium of the forces of evil than it is to put oneself at the disposition of the Force of Good. "There are a group of people ... who want to create a kind of religion based on the revelation of Sri Aurobindo. But they have taken only the side of power and force, a certain kind of knowledge and all that could be utilised by Asuric forces. There is a big Asuric being that has succeeded in taking the appearance of Sri Aurobindo ... This appearance of Sri Aurobindo has declared that I have been a traitor to him and to his work, and has refused to have anything to do with me."[20] It is not difficult to imagine the religion the Mother here

---

19. See the chapter "The Lord of the Nations" in *Beyond Man*.
20. *Words of the Mother*, CWM 15, p. 408.

talks about: one has only to think of the superman as conceived by Friedrich Nietzsche.

"I am no longer in my body. I have left it for the Lord to take care of it, to decide if it is to have the Supramental or not. I know and I have said also that now is the last fight. If the purpose for which this body is alive is to be fulfilled, that is to say, *the first steps taken towards the Supramental transformation,* then it will continue today. That is the Lord's decision. I am not even asking what he has decided. If the body is incapable of bearing the fight, if it has to be dissolved, then humanity will pass through a critical time. What the Asuric Force that has succeeded in taking the appearance of Sri Aurobindo will create is a new religion or thought, perhaps cruel and merciless, in the name of the Supramental Realisation." When the transcript of this talk was read to the Mother on one of the following days, she commented: "The fight is within the body. This can't go on. They must be defeated or this body is defeated. All depends on what the Lord will decide. It [her body] is the battlefield ..."

"Several weeks of grave illness threatened the Mother's life",[21] read the introductory words to the following bulletin: "Suddenly in the night I woke with the full awareness of what we could call the Yoga of the World. The Supreme Love was manifesting through big pulsations, and each pulsation was bringing the world further in its manifestation. It was the formidable pulsations of the eternal stupendous Love, only Love ...

"And there was the certitude that what was to be one is done[22] and that the Supramental Manifestation is realised.

"Everything was personal, nothing was individual.[23]

"This was going on, and on, and on, and on.

"The certitude that what was to be done *is done* ..."[24]

---

21. Ibid., pp. 411-12.
22. The text reads here "that what is to be done is done", but this is in obvious contradiction to the meaning of the whole, spoken in English by the Mother and possibly misunderstood by the French disciple, Pavitra, who noted it down.
23. The Mother apparently means that everything was an experience of her universal personality as the Universal Mother, not of her physical incarnation on the earth.
24. *Words of the Mother,* CWM 15, pp. 411-12 (first and second emphases added).

6. The Consciousness of the Overman

The Sixties

The Sixties were happening. The Twentieth Century, the most surprising, eventful and bloody century in human history, was taking a turn towards the unknown. The Mother said: "According to what I am being told – I mean by people who listen to the radio and read newspapers, all things I never do – the whole world seems to be undergoing an action which for the moment is disconcerting ... In America, for instance, the entire youth seems to be in the grip of a sort of curious vertigo, disconcerting to reasonable people but certainly an indication that an unusual force is at work. It implies the breaking of all habits and all rules. It is good. It may be somewhat strange for the time being, but it is necessary ...

"The best one can do is not to have any prejudices, not to have preconceived ideas or principles – you know: the moral principles, the preconceptions concerning the rules of conduct, what one must do and what one must not do, and the preconceived ideas concerning morality, concerning progress, and all the social and mental conventions. There is no worse obstacle ...

"To stick to something one believes one knows, to stick to the way one feels, to stick to what one loves, to stick to one's habits, to stick to one's supposed needs, to stick to the world as it is: that is what ties you down. You must undo all that, one thing after the other. All the ties must be undone. We have said this thousands of times and the people continue all the same. Even those who are most eloquent and preach this to others, how they remain stuck: they stick to their way of seeing, their way of feeling, their habit of progress, which seems to them the only one. No more ties – free! free! Always ready to change, except one thing: to aspire, to thirst.

"I understand it well, there are people who do not like the idea of a 'Godhead' because it gets immediately mixed up with all kinds of European or Occidental conceptions which are terrible, and this complicates their life to some extent. But one does not need that! What one needs is the Light, what one needs is the Love, what one needs is the Truth, what one needs is the supreme Perfection, and nothing else! Formulas ... the fewer formulas there are, the better. But this: a need which *That* alone can satisfy. Nothing else, no half-measures: *That* alone. And then: godspeed! Whatever your way, it does not matter. It does not matter! Even the extravagances of the modern American youth may be a way. It does not matter."[25] The radical spirit of the beginning had, if possible, grown still more radical. The Mother founded Auroville on 28 February 1968. The principles of this Utopian "City of Dawn" were those of the Integral Yoga, and so was its goal. Then how did it differ from the Sri Aurobindo Ashram? It might be put as follows: the tender shoot of the Integral Yoga planted in the well-protected greenhouse of the Ashram had flourished into a strong young tree. Now the time had come to plant a first shoot of this tree in the open territory of the world. In the 'Charter of Auroville', a universal township-to-be which started from nothing in the middle of nowhere, the Mother wrote that the new city "belongs to nobody in particular", but "to humanity as a whole"; that it would be "the place of unending education, of constant progress, and a youth that never ages"; that it "wants to be the bridge between the past and the future"; and that it "will be a site of spiritual and material researches for a living embodiment of an actual Human Unity".

However, the key to the whole charter and therefore to Auroville was contained in its first paragraph: "To live in Auroville one must be the willing servitor of the Divine Consciousness". The Mother was, of course, very much aware that this was the touchstone of the whole enterprise. No wonder then that from the very beginning, even before Auroville's inauguration, the squabbling started precisely over this point. Which Divine? Which Divine Consciousness? Were the vision and the teachings of Sri Aurobindo and the Mother to be accepted in order to be an Aurovillian? Were Sri Aurobindo and the Mother to be accepted as the Divine? How can one formulate things like that without making a religion out of it? And so on.

---

25. The Mother: *Notes on the Way*, pp. 1, 6-7.

6. The Consciousness of the Overman

No doubt, the Mother foresaw it all: the material difficulties to be conquered in a very tough terrain; the spiritual ignorance and confusion; the egos of the individuals and the different groups – national, racial, cultural, and others – dancing their dances; the cultural and financial problems. Sri Aurobindo and the Mother herself had already pointed out on several occasions that the chief condition for the overman and the superman to come into being was an invincible occult protection against all the visible and occult influences which would try to make their presence impossible. Auroville was to be "the cradle of the superman", wrote the Mother; this implied that, for the time being, it was also to be the cradle of the overman. The fact that after thirty-two years it is not only still there but even growing and expanding is proof that a Force is very concretely protecting it, for otherwise the whole project would have come to nothing because of its internal and external tribulations.

Perhaps the power poured into the atmosphere of the earth to establish Auroville caused a chain reaction elsewhere. Nanterre University, in the suburbs of Paris, was occupied by the students on 22 March 1968. And after March followed "May '68", with the barricades: in Paris and repercussions all over the globe. And there was the Prague Spring, when a few intellectuals stood up against a communist totalitarianism. A spirit of freedom, novelty, daring, improvisation and hankering for something better because more authentic, more honest, more sincere, wandered over the planet and inspired hundreds and thousands who never fully realised what was driving them. One cannot but recall the Mother's prophetic insight when she said some four years earlier: "In America, for instance, the entire youth seems to be in the grip of a sort of curious vertigo, disconcerting to reasonable people but certainly an indication that an unusual force is at work ..."

She followed the events with keen interest. She said that it was "the highest Power" that forced the people to do what they had to do, and: "This has not at all the character of a strike, it has the character of a revolution ... It is clearly the future that is awakening and that wants to chase away the past."[26] These words sounded almost pitifully inflated when after a few days the student's movement in Paris fizzled out, when the wild waves abated everywhere, and still more when in the following years most grandiloquent leaders of the events fell in step with the establishment. At that time "May '68" was "cruelly vilified" (Bernard-Henri Lévy) by the media.

But not any longer. For its importance has gradually grown evident and now even academic historians (like Eric Hobsbawn) concede that it was in the Sixties that the century took an unexpected turn into a future which nobody is yet able to interpret.

But: what has all this to do with overman? Everything. For there is no doubt that the external global events were the physical expression of the ongoing spiritual transformation. Sri Aurobindo once wrote that the French Revolution of 1789 was made possible because of the *siddhi* of Freedom, Equality and Brotherhood realised by some unknown yogi in the Himalayas. ("If the French Revolution took place, it was because a soul on the Indian snows dreamed of God as freedom, brotherhood and equality."[27]) An Avatar has more power than a yogi; he does not come to write great literature or say impressive things and build castles in the air, but to change an era. Speaking of overman, a surprise was in store.

"There are Some ..."

Discussing the constitution of the supramental being, the Mother said on 30 September 1966: "This would be a transformation that is infinitely greater than that from the animal into man: this would be a change from man into a being no longer built in the same way, no longer functioning in the same way, being as it were a condensation or concretisation of something ... Up to the present, this corresponds to nothing we have yet seen physically, unless the scientists have found something

---

26. *Mother's Agenda,* 22 May 1968.
27. Sri Aurobindo: *Essays Divine and Human,* p. 460.

6. The Consciousness of the Overman

I do not know of ... It is the leap, you see, that seems so enormous to me. I conceive without difficulty of a being that could, by spiritual power, the power of its inner being, absorb the necessary forces, renew itself and remain always young. One conceives this without any difficulty, even that some suppleness can be given to change the form if need be. But the total disappearance of this system of construction [of the body] all at once – all at once, from one [being] to the other? ... It seems to require stages."[28]

She continued to reflect on this. "How long would it take to do away with the necessity – let us consider this problem only – of the skeleton? This seems to me still very far away in the future." The physical substance required for the functioning of the supramental body would have to be of a kind "that I do not know. It is not the substance as we know it now, and it is surely not the [bodily] construction that we know now ... It seems to me that between what exists at present, the way we are, and that other form of life, many intermediary stages will be needed ... It is something I feel more and more: the necessity of intermediary periods. It is quite obvious that something is happening, but it is not the 'something' that was seen and foreseen, and that will be the final accomplishment [i.e. the supramental being]. It is one of the [intermediary] stages that is going to happen, it is not the final accomplishment."[29]

Then, on the first day of the year 1969 something "new" happened. "During the night it was coming slowly, and on waking up in the morning there was as it were a golden dawn, and the atmosphere was very light. The[30] body felt: 'Hey, this is really, really new.' A golden light, imponderous and benevolent – benevolent in the sense of a certitude, a harmonious certitude. It was new. *Voilà*. And when I say *'bonne année'* to the people, it is that that I pass on to them. And this morning I have spent

---

28. The Mother: *Notes on the Way*, pp. 46-47.
29. Ibid., pp. 55 ff. passim.
30. Since the great experience of April 1962, the Mother considered her body as *a* body that she had taken up to continue the Work.

my time like this, spontaneously, saying: *'Bonne année, bonne année ...'"*

The Mother never mentally dissected her experiences immediately after they had happened. She let them develop and take their complete shape so that she could be sure of their meaning, of their portent. We will follow the process in this case. On 4 January, she said: "On the 1st something really strange happened. And I was not the only one to feel it, several other persons felt it too. It was just after midnight [i.e. the beginning of the new year], but I felt it at two o'clock and others felt it at four o'clock in the morning. Last time I spoke to you about it in passing, but what is surprising is that it had absolutely nothing to do with anything I was expecting – I was expecting nothing – or with other things which I had felt [coming] ...

"My impression was that of an immense personality. Immense! By this I mean that, compared to it, the earth was small, small like this *(gesture as if holding a small ball in the palm of her hand)*, like a ball. An immense personality, very, very benevolent, that came in order to – *(Mother does as if she gently lifts up a small ball in the palm of her hand).* The impression was of a personal godhead ... who comes to help. And so strong, so strong and at the same time so gentle, so comprehending ...

"It was luminous, smiling, and so benevolent *because of its power.* By this I mean that, generally speaking, benevolence in the human being is something rather weak, in the sense that it does not like combat, it does not like fighting. This is nothing of the sort! [It is] a benevolence that imposes itself *(Mother brings her fists down upon the armrests of her chair)* ... What is it? ... Since its coming, the feeling of the body is of a kind of certitude, a certitude as if now it no longer has the anxiety or uncertainty of needing to know: 'How will it be like? What will the Supramental be like – *physically*, what will it be like physically?' That was what the body asked itself. Now it does not think of that any more, it is satisfied ...

"I have the feeling that it is the formation that is going to enter, that is going to express itself – to enter and express itself – in what will be the bodies of the Supramental. Or perhaps ... the

6. The Consciousness of the Overman

overman *[le surhomme]*[31] don't know. The intermediary between the two [between man and superman]. Perhaps the overman. It was very human, but human with divine proportions, you see. Human without weaknesses and without shadows: it was all light, all light and smiling, and sweetness at the same time. Yes, perhaps the overman."[32]

Finally, on 8 January, she identified the new Consciousness: "It is the descent of the consciousness of the overman *[le surhomme]*. I had the assurance afterwards. It was 1 January, after midnight. I woke up at two in the morning, surrounded by a consciousness, so concrete and so *new*, by which I mean that I had never felt that before. And it lasted, absolutely concrete, *there*, for two or three hours. And afterwards it spread out and went in search of all the people who were able to receive it. And I knew that it was the consciousness of the overman, that is to say: the intermediary between man and the supramental being. This has given to the body a kind of assurance, of confidence. It is as if this experience stabilised it [the body], and, if it keeps the right attitude, as if every support is there to help it."[33]

Ten days later, on 18 January, the Mother had become quite familiar with the new Consciousness: "Well, it is very consciously active. It is like a projection of power. And it has now become habitual. There is a consciousness in it – something *very* precious – that gives lessons to the body, teaching it what it must do, that is to say which attitude it must take, which reaction it must have. I had told you many times that it is very difficult to find the process of transformation when there is nobody to give you any indications. Well, it is as if this were the reply. It comes and tells the body: 'Take this attitude, do this, do that in that way.' And so the body is content, it is completely reassured, it can no longer be mistaken. It is very interesting. It came as a mentor – *practical*, completely practical … In one of the former *Entretiens*, when I spoke there at the Playground, I said: 'No doubt, the overman will be in the first place a being of

---

31. Here again *surhomme* has each time been translated by "superman".
32. The Mother: *Notes on the Way*, pp. 149 ff.
33. Ibid., p. 153 (emphasis in the text).

power, so that he may defend himself.' Well, this is it, it is that experience. It came back as an experience. And it is because it came back as an experience that I remember having said it."[34]

We may draw some conclusions from these words with their far-reaching implications. Overman is the intermediary being between man and superman, and his job is to make the supramental being possible, to find the means of producing the supramental body that will be the crown of Sri Aurobindo and the Mother's Yoga – and of the Yoga of all those who work towards the same aim, who are "looking in the same direction" as the Mother put it. This, however, does not mean that the Consciousness of the overman is less than the supramental Consciousness. The latter having been established in the atmosphere of the earth in 1956, it would make no sense for a lesser consciousness to become active in the ongoing process of supramentalisation. The Consciousness of the overman is an *aspect* of the supramental Consciousness: it *is* the supramental Consciousness that emanates itself in a certain way in order to accomplish a certain task, namely the formation of the overman.

Two facts make this very clear. Firstly, the consciousness of the intermediary being that is overman is a supramental consciousness, called by Sri Aurobindo "the Mind of Light". The fact that he defined it as the lowest degree of the Supermind does not diminish its importance. *Any* degree of the Supermind is supramental; anything supramental is divine; anything divine is worlds above our human status. Secondly, in 1969 the Mother was already far advanced in the realisation of the supramental body within her gross material body. Therefore the fact that she was so plainly content with the presence and guidance of the Consciousness of the overman, acting as her mentor, is a sure indication of its supramental status.

The presence of the Consciousness of the overman in the atmosphere of the earth is a permanent fact, whether it is known or not. It means that overmen and overwomen are coming into existence and are already there, now, unnoticed, in the common

---

34. The Mother: *Notes on the Way,* pp. 154-55 (emphasis in the text).

6. The Consciousness of the Overman

mass of humanity. The Mother herself has pointed this out when she said in April 1972: "The change from the human into the supramental being is being achieved ... through the overman. It may be that there will be some overmen – *there are some* – who will make the transition possible."[35]

Another relevant reference in this connection is found in one of the very last *Entretiens* which is dated fourteen years earlier: "All those who make an effort to overcome their ordinary nature, all those who try to realise materially the profound experience that has brought them into contact with the divine Truth, all those who, instead of turning to the Hereafter or the On-high, try to realise physically, externally, the change of consciousness they have realised within themselves – all those are apprentice-overmen *[des apprentis-surhommes]*. Among them, there are countless variations according to the success of their efforts. Each time we try not to be an ordinary man, not to live the ordinary life, to express in our movements, our actions and reactions the divine Truth, when we are governed by that Truth instead of being governed by the general ignorance, we are apprentice-overmen, and according to the success of our efforts we are, well, more or less good apprentices, more or less advanced on the way."[36]

The Mother would continue her sometimes ecstatic, often gruesome, but always glorious Yoga of the body till the end on 17 November 1973, at the time of writing twenty-seven years ago. Gradually the prototype of the supramental body took shape in her in a series of extraordinary experiences. She saw her new body in May 1970, and *ce n'était pas surhumain,* it was not a body of the overman but of the superman. In March 1972 the formation of the supramental body was complete: she was like that, she said, she "had a totally new body". But this is outside the compass of this essay and has been narrated elsewhere.

The twentieth century has seen such a storm of upheaval that the learned have run out of explanations. Our world, our planet is going through an unprecedented crisis; all are agreed

---

35. *Mother's Agenda*, 15 April 1972.
36. The Mother: *Questions and Answers 1957-58*, p. 411.

that something singular is happening, but nobody has any notion what that something might be. This is not unusual: mankind has never known the deeper rationale of the throes it was subject to, except *post factum,* and the exceptional beings who did know have never been believed. Why should it be otherwise this time? "Most people are blind", said the Mother, "they will go till the end without seeing anything. But those who have their eyes open will see."[37] In order to see, however, there is a condition: that we change from a blind species into a species which has its inner sight activated – that the darkness of our mind changes into a Mind of Light. All remains literature and fantasy stuff unless we become apprentice-overmen and apprentice-overwomen. "There are some ..."

Auroville, 28 March 2001

---

37. *Mother's Agenda,* 18 May 1968.

Note About the Sources

The first edition of Sri Aurobindo's writings was published thirty years ago, in view of his birth centenary in 1972, and appropriately called "Sri Aurobindo Birth Centenary Library" (SABCL).

At the time of writing this book, a new revised and augmented edition of Sri Aurobindo's writings is being published: "The Complete Works of Sri Aurobindo" (CWSA), but many volumes of this new edition are still awaiting publication.

This puts the writer in the uncomfortable position of having to quote from two sets of Sri Aurobindo's works. The reader interested in retracing the sources should therefore know to which set of works the quoted writings belong.

To the "Sri Aurobindo Birth Centenary Library" belong:

Collected Poems (vol. 5)
The Upanishads (vol. 12)
The Life Divine (vol. 18 and 19)
Letters on Yoga (vol. 22, 23 and 24)
On the Mother (vol. 25)
On Himself (vol. 26).

To "The Complete Works of Sri Aurobindo" belong:

Essays Divine and Human (vol. 12)
Essays in Philosophy and Yoga (vol. 13)
Essays on the Gita (vol. 19)
The Synthesis of Yoga (vol. 23 and 24)
The Human Cycle (vol. 25)
Savitri (vol. 33 and 34).

All quoted works of the Mother belong to the centenary edition of the "Collected Works of the Mother" (CWM), and have been checked against the original French edition.

The two sets of Collected Works are available online at:
www.sriaurobindoashram.org/ashram/sriauro/writings.php
www.sriaurobindoashram.org/ashram/mother/writings.php

Biographical Note

Georges Van Vrekhem (°1935) is a Flemish speaking Belgian who writes in English. He became known in his country as a journalist, poet and playwright. For some time he was the artistic manager of a professional theatre company. He gave numerous talks and presentations in America, Europe and India.

He became first acquainted with the works of Sri Aurobindo and the Mother in 1964. In 1970 he joined the Sri Aurobindo Ashram in Pondicherry, and in 1978 he became a member of Auroville, where he is still living and writing.

He wrote:

Beyond Man, the Life and Work of Sri Aurobindo and The Mother (1997)

The Mother, the Story of Her Life (2000)

Overman, the Intermediary between the Human and the Supramental Being (2000)

Patterns of the Present, in the Light of Sri Aurobindo and the Mother (2001)

The Mother: the Divine Shakti (2003)

Hitler and his God – The Background to the Nazi Phenomenon (2006)

Evolution, Religion, and the Unknown God (2011)

Books by him are translated into Dutch, French, German, Italian, Russian, and Spanish. He was awarded the Sri Aurobindo Puraskar for 2006 by the Government of Bengal.

Printed in Great Britain
by Amazon